American Indian
Athletic
Hall of Fame

1972-2009

Order this book online at www.trafford.com
or email orders@trafford.com

Most Trafford titles are also available at major online book retailers.

Printed in Victoria, BC, Canada.

ISBN: 978-1-4269-2379-1 (sc)
ISBN: 978-1-4269-2380-7 (hc)

Library of Congress Control Number: 2009913518

*Our mission is to efficiently provide the world's finest, most comprehensive book publishing
service, enabling every author to experience success. To find out how to publish your book, your
way, and have it available worldwide, visit us online at www.trafford.com*

Trafford rev. 01/06/10

North America & international
toll-free: 1 888 232 4444 (USA & Canada)
phone: 250 383 6864 ♦ fax: 812 355 4082

Contents

PREFACE

The American Indian Athletic Hall of Fame is a non-profit corporation originally organized under the statutes of the State of Kansas in 1972. It was brought into existence by a constituency of Indian leaders and under the leadership and direction of Mr. Robert L. Bennett, (Oneida) former Commissioner of the Bureau of Indian Affairs and Mr. Louis R. Bruce, (Mohawk) also a former Commissioner of the Bureau of Indian Affairs.

The purpose of the Hall of Fame is to recognize and pay tribute to American Indian athletes for their achievements and to preserve a permanent record of their attainments. The Hall of Fame is currently located on the campus of Haskell Indian Nations University in Lawrence, Kansas. A bronze plaque bearing an etched photograph with the inscription of outstanding achievements of each person inducted is on display on the campus. If you know of American Indian athletes whom you believe the Board of Directors should consider for induction into the American Indian Athletic Hall of Fame complete the Application found at the end of this book. Mail completed applications to Board of Directors, American Indian Athletic Hall of Fame, 1827 E. Saint Charles Ave., Phoenix, Arizona 85042. Include a photograph of the nominee in his or her sports uniform, newspaper clippings, record book documentation and any other pertinent data reflecting outstanding achievements or awards as an athlete. The Board of Directors will consider and evaluate all applications.

The first induction was held in 1972 in Lawrence, Kansas, when fourteen athletes were enshrined in the Hall of Fame. Since that time the Hall has grown to house over 90 inductees, representing fifty-four American Indian Tribes. To date twenty different sport categories have been recognized. This book gives you a brief overview of the inductees' athletic accomplishments. You will find this to be a one of a kind book, written with permission of the American Indian Athletic Hall of Fame Board of Directors. All proceeds will go to benefit future induction ceremonies for the Hall of Fame.

1972 INDUCTION

LAWRENCE, KANSAS

Alexander Arcasa

ALEXANDER ARCASA
Inducted 1972

DATE OF BIRTH: March 24, 1890

DATE OF DEATH: September 6, 1962

BIRTH PLACE: Orient, Washington

TRIBE: Colville

EDUCATION: Carlisle Indian School 1909-1912

SPORTS DATA: Football – Halfback

Lacrosse

ACHIEVEMENTS:

- Football: Named to Walter Camp's All-American team of 1912. He was Camp's second choice after Jim Thorpe.

- Lacrosse: Captain-Carlisle had best Lacrosse team in the nation in 1912.

COMMENTS:

- Named to the Inland Empire Sports Hall of Fame

- November 9, 1912 Carlisle played Army bidding for national Honors. Army scored first, but the rest of the day belonged to Arcasa. Playing the greatest game of his career Arcasa scored three touchdowns as Carlisle won, 27-6. Playing fullback on the great Army team was Dwight Eisenhower.

Charles Bender

CHARLES A. "CHIEF" BENDER
Inducted 1972

DATE OF BIRTH: May 5, 1884

DATE OF DEATH: May 22, 1954

BIRTH PLACE: Brainerd, Minnesota

TRIBE: Chippewa

EDUCATION: Carlisle Indian School 1902

SPORTS DATA: Baseball

ACHIEVEMENTS:

- Professional Baseball pitcher for Philadelphia, American League

- Pitched no-hitter against Cleveland, May 12, 1910

- Pitched no-hitter against Bridgeport, August 19, 1920

- Pitched in World Series; 1905-1910-1911-1913-1914

COMMENTS:

Coached:

- Chicago White Sox, 1925-1926

- Philadelphia Athletics, 1951-1953

- Named to the Baseball Hall of Fame 1953

Wilson Charles

WILSON D. "BUSTER" CHARLES
Inducted 1972

DATE OF BIRTH: April 4, 1908

DATE OF DEATH: November 26, 1952

BIRTH PLACE: Green Bay, Wisconsin

TRIBE: Oneida

EDUCATION: Haskell Indian School 1928-1932

    University of New Mexico

SPORTS DATA: Track & Field – Decathlon

ACHIEVEMENTS:

- Decathlon Champion Kansas Relays 1930

- National AAU Decathlon Champion 1930 (all events being held in one day)

- Member of the United States Olympic Team in 1932; 4th place Olympic Games Decathlon

- South Dakota Hall of Fame Member 1968

QUOTES:

Buster Charles was feted as the Nation's Greatest Athlete at a Chamber of Commerce banquet in Lawrence, Kansas.

Albert Exendine

ALBERT A. EXENDINE
Inducted 1972

DATE OF BIRTH: January 27, 1884

DATEOF DEATH: January 4, 1973

BIRTH PLACE: Bartlesville, Oklahoma

TRIBE: Delaware

EDUCATION: Carlisle Indian School 1902-1907

SPORTS DATA: Football – End

ACHIEVEMENTS:

- All-American recognition as an End in 1906 and 1907

- Inducted into College Football Hall of Fame 1970

COMMENTS:

An outstanding career as a coach:

- Carlisle 1908-1913

- Georgetown University 1914-1922

- Washington State University 1923-1925

- Oklahoma State University 1934-1935
  Formerly Oklahoma A&M College

Joseph Guyon

JOSEPH N. GUYON
Inducted 1972

DATE OF BIRTH: November 26, 1892

DATE OF DEATH: November 1, 1971

BIRTH PLACE: White Earth, Minnesota

TRIBE: White Earth Chippewa

EDUCATION: Carlisle Indian School 1911-1912

Georgia Tech University, 1917-1918

SPORTS DATA: Football

ACHIEVEMENTS:

College Athletics:

- Football – Tackle and Halfback

- All-American, All-Indian Backfield, Carlisle 1913-1914

- All-American Tackle, 1917 Georgia Tech

- All-American Halfback, 1918 Georgia Tech

Professional Athletics - Football:

- Canton Bulldogs, 1919-1921 & 1923-1924

- Ooran Indians, 1922

- Kansas City Cowboys, 1925-1926

- New York Giants, 1927

- National Professional Football Hall of Fame, 1966

QUOTES:

Grantland Rice, Dean of American Sportswriters, once wrote, "I believe an All-American, All-Indian Football team could beat the All-Time Notre Dame Team, the All-Time Michigan Team, or the All-Time anything else. Take a look at a backfield like Jim Thorpe, Joe Guyon, Pete Calac and Frank Mount Pleasant."

Jimmie Johnson

JIMMIE JOHNSON
Inducted 1972

DATE OF BIRTH: June 6, 1879

DATE OF DEATH: January, 1942

BIRTH PLACE: Edgerton, Wisconsin

TRIBE: Stockbridge – Munsee

EDUCATION: Carlisle Indian School 1899-1903

                  Northwestern University 1904-1905

SPORTS DATA: Football

ACHIEVEMENTS:

- Football – Carlisle Quarterback 1899-1903

- 1903 Carlisle wins 10 games

- Walter Camps 1903 All-American Football Team

- "Hidden ball trick" against Harvard became a legendary story about Pop Warner.

- Defeated Northwestern 28-0 in final game of 1903 season.

- 1904 Enrolls in Northwestern Dental School – Plays quarterback for two seasons, 1904-1905. (Until 1906 it was legal for a school to play graduate students even though they had played four years somewhere else.)

- Named Captain of Northwestern team.

- Led Northwestern to 16 wins, 1 tie, 4 losses.

- Member of College Football Hall of Fame.

COMMENTS:

Johnson was not big but he was cunning and shrewd, an excellent field goal kicker and a great leader. He was a great improviser and was the quarterback who called the huddle and ran the football inside the back of Dillon's Jersey against Harvard in 1903.

Following graduation he remained at Carlisle as Assistant Coach until 1904, when he entered Northwestern University and graduated from the School of Dentistry.

John Levi

JOHN LEVI

Inducted 1972

DATE OF BIRTH: June 14, 1898

DATE OF DEATH: 1946

BIRTH PLACE: Bridgeport, Oklahoma

TRIBE: Arapaho

EDUCATION: Haskell Indian School

SPORTS DATA: Football

ACHIEVEMENTS:

- All-American Football – Fullback 1923

- Professional Baseball – New York Yankees

- Coached Football at Haskell 1926-1936

QUOTE:

- Jim Thorpe says of John Levi: He is the greatest Athlete I have ever seen.

- Minneapolis Tribune: He is 20 years old. He is six feet two inches tall and like all Indian Athletes is wiry and sinewy and carries no useless flesh. He weighs an even two hundred pounds, and it is all "fighting weight".

COMMENTS: From James Houston Turner "Big John"

- "The great Jim Thorpe stands tall and first in the line of football legends. But Thorpe knew someone who was better! His Arapaho name meant Charging Buffalo, but to those on the campus of Haskell Indian Institute, John Levi was known simply as "Skee." To everyone else, he is remembered as BIG JOHN."

- "The Story: voted first team All-American fullback his junior year, Olympic hopeful John Levi looked poised to surpass Thorpe's amazing athletic accomplishments. But not everyone was happy with Levi's success. By defeating nearly every team they played, Haskell – a tiny remedial Indian school in the mud flats of eastern Kansas – had become a threat to the nation's prestigious university athletic system. They had to be stopped. And Levi was the key. What followed was Levi's heart-rending triumph over incredible odds, including one of the most extraordinary actual football games *never* recorded."

John Meyers

JOHN MEYERS
Inducted 1972

DATE OF BIRTH: July 29, 1880

DATE OF DEATH: July 25, 1971

BIRTH PLACE: Riverside (Cahiulla Village), California

TRIBE: Cahiulla Band

EDUCATION: Riverside High School

                    Dartmouth College

SPORTS DATA: Baseball – Catcher

ACHIEVEMENTS:

- Professional: Major League Baseball Teams
  New York Giants, 1908 (1911-1913, batted .332, .358 & .312)
  Brooklyn Dodgers, 1916

- Lifetime major league batting average of .291

- Held a World Series record for most assists (12) by a catcher
  in a six game series

- Earned the title of "Ironman" behind plate during 1911-1913

- Semi-pro Manager: New Haven, 1917

COMMENTS:

Out of respect for John T Meyers as exemplified by the following quote from 'Baseball Library.com', The American Indian Athletic Hall of Fame has left the term 'Chief' from his bylines.

- "A Cahuilla Indian from California, Meyers was the New York Giants' star catcher when they won three straight pennants from 1911 to 1913; he batted .332, .358, and .312 in those years. Slowed by catching more than 100 games in six straight seasons (1910-15), he retired at age 37 in 1917. He was booed while managing in a semi-pro game in 1920 and, disgusted, quit baseball. Educated at Dartmouth, he was employed by the Department of the Interior as an Indian supervisor. He scoffed at his nickname, Chief, bestowed on virtually every athlete of Indian ancestry".

- From 'Legends of the Game' (www.deadball.com/meyers.htm) "Chief's .291 career batting average was the highest for catchers playing during this 'dead ball' era. He was the battery mate of HOF legend, Christy Mathewson on the powerhouse, NY Giants. Meyers was also roomed with a teammate considered the greatest athlete of the first 50 years of the 20th century, Jim Thorpe. During the 1911 World Series Classic, Chief established a series record by throwing out 12 runners in 6 games."

Allie Reynolds

ALLIE P. REYNOLDS
Inducted 1972

DATE OF BIRTH: February 10, 1917

DATE OF DEATH: December 26, 1994

BIRTH PLACE: Bethany, Oklahoma

TRIBE: Creek

EDUCATION: Oklahoma City Capitol Hill High School
                   1933-1934

                   Oklahoma State University, 1935-1939

SPORTS DATA: Track, Football, Baseball

ACHIEVEMENTS:

College Athletic Achievements:

- No hit baseball game 1938

- High Point honors in 1935 track meet

Professional Baseball Achievements: Pitcher

- New York Sports Writers Player of the Year, Sid Mercer Award, 1951

- Led American League in strikeouts, 1943 and 1952

- Best Earned Run average, American League, 1952

- Pitched Most Shutouts, American League, 1945 and 1952

- All-American – All-Professional, 1952

- Professional Athlete of the Year, 1951

- Tied World's Record – World series Wins

- Two no-hit games, 1951 (first in history of American League)

- Pitched 37 shutouts (second among modern players)

- Champion in the 1952 National Baseball Players Golf Tournament

- Oklahoma Baseball Hall of Fame, 1956

- American League All-Star Team 1943, 1947, 1951-1954

- President – American Association of Professional Baseball Clubs, 1969 -1971

COMMENTS:

On August 26, 1989, the Yankees dedicated a plaque in Reynolds' honor, to hang in Monument part at Yankee Stadium. Reynolds and several of his Yankee teammates, including Mickey Mantle, Whitey Ford and Phil Rizzuto, were on hand. The plaque calls him "One of the Yankees' greatest right-handed pitchers."

Theodore Roebuck

THEODORE "TINY" ROEBUCK
Inducted 1972

DATE OF BIRTH: January 26, 1906

DATE OF DEATH: June 1, 1969

BIRTH PLACE: Lenton Indian Territory (Choctaw Nation)

TRIBE: Choctaw

EDUCATION: Haskell Institute – 1926

SPORTS DATA: Football

ACHIEVEMENTS:

- Football – Tackle

- All-State 1926

- All-Western Tackle

- All-American Tackle – 1926

- East-West Charity Football Game – 1926

Reuben Sanders

RUEBEN SANDERS

Inducted 1972

DATE OF BIRTH: July 10, 1876

DATE OF DEATH: December 20, 1957

BIRTH PLACE: Corvallis, Oregon

TRIBE: Tututni/Rogue River Indian

EDUCATION: Chemawa Indian School

SPORTS DATA: Football – Halfback

ACHIEVEMENTS:

Teams Sanders Played For:

- Chemawa Indian School

- Willamette College – four years

- Multnomah Amateur Athletic Club

- Salem Capital Athletic Club

COMMENTS:

Rueben Sanders is described as being one of the State of Oregon's greatest All-Time Football Players and All-Around Athletes. He was a veritable plague to University of Oregon teams of his period. In those not too strict eligibility days, Sanders played against the University of Oregon team, four times during one season, representing four different teams. He was inducted into the State of Oregon Athletic Hall of Fame in 1999.

Louis Tewanima

LOUIS TEWANIMA
Inducted 1972

DATE OF BIRTH: January 1, 1878

DATE OF DEATH: January 18, 1969

BIRTH PLACE: Second Mesa, Arizona

TRIBE: Hopi

EDUCATION: Carlisle Indian School 1907-1912

SPORTS DATA: Track

ACHIEVEMENTS:

- Track, Distance Runner

- Member of the 1908 Olympic Team

- Member of the 1912 Olympic Team; 2nd Place Olympic 10,000 meters

- Helms Foundation Member to the All-Time US Track and Field Team 1954

- Arizona Sports Hall of Fame Member 1957

- Established a new World Record in the ten mile run 1909

QUOTE:

- From Indigenous Voices of the Colorado Plateau: Tewanima "was a member of the 1908 and 1912 United States Olympic track teams. In the 1908 games, he placed 9th in the marathon. In 1912, he won a silver medal and established a record that stood for 52 years until it was broken by another Native American team member. Tewanima was educated at the Carlisle Boarding School in Carlisle, Pennsylvania. Stories tell of Tewanima running 120 miles from his home on the Hopi Mesas to the town of Winslow, Arizona in one day, just to watch the trains pass. At school in Carlisle, he once missed the train to a track meet and ran eighteen miles to the meet, where he placed second in the two mile event."

- Jim Thorpe writing in 1940 remembered: "I recall the day Carlisle had a dual meet with the Lafayette College 20 man team. We had only three Indians (Thorpe, Frank Mount Pleasant and Louis Tewanima), Tewanima's reply was; 'Me run fast good …. All Hopis run fast good.' Almost immediately, Tewanima proceeded to clean up everything America had to offer in the 10-mile and 15-mile races."

Jim Thorpe

JIM THORPE
Inducted 1972

DATE OF BIRTH: May 28, 1888

DATE OF DEATH: March 28, 1953

BIRTH PLACE: Prague, Oklahoma

TRIBE: Potawatomi/Sac & Fox

EDUCATION: Carlisle Indian School

    Cumberland Valley College

SPORTS DATA: Track and Field

    Football

ACHIEVEMENTS:

College Athletic Achievements:

- All-American halfback – Carlisle 1908

- All-American halfback – Carlisle 1911 - 1912

- Gold Medal winner in the Pentathlon and the Decathlon at the 1912 Olympic Games

Professional Achievements:

- Football – 1920-1929 with the Canton Bulldogs and the New York Giants.

- First President of the American Football Association which became the National Football League

- Major League Baseball – played minor and major league baseball for 20 years including New York Giants, Boston Braves and the Cincinnati Reds

QUOTE:

- The King of Sweden as he congratulated Jim Thorpe on winning the Olympic Decathlon, "You sir are the greatest Athlete in the World."

- 1950 Jim Thorpe was voted the greatest Athlete of the 1st half century.

- 1963 Elected to the Pro-Football National Hall of Fame.

- *Wikipedia Encyclopedia* "Jim" Thorpe is considered one of the most versatile athletes in modern sports. He won Olympic gold medals in the pentathlon and decathlon, starred in college and professional football, played Major League Baseball and also had a career in basketball. He subsequently lost his Olympic titles when it was found he had played two seasons of minor league baseball prior to competing in the games (thus violating the amateur status rules). In 1983, thirty years after his death, his medals were restored.

- *Wikipedia Encyclopedia* "A ticket discovered in an old book recently brought to light his career in basketball. Jim Thorpe and His World-Famous Indians barnstormed for at least two years (1927-1928) in parts of New York, Pennsylvania, and Marion, Ohio. Although images of Thorpe in his WFI basketball uniform were printed on postcards and published in newspapers, this period of his life was not well-documented, and until 2005 most of Thorpe's biographers were unaware of his basketball career."

Louis Weller

LOUIS "RABBIT" WELLER
Inducted 1972

DATE OF BIRTH: March 2, 1904

DATE OF DEATH: April, 1979

BIRTH PLACE: Anadarko, Oklahoma

TRIBE: Caddo

EDUCATION: Haskell Institute, Lawrence, Kansas

SPORTS DATA: Football (Track, Baseball, Basketball)

ACHIEVEMENTS:

- Football:

  All-State, Kansas – four years

  Team two-years

- Honorary Teams:

  No. 1 All-Western Team chosen by Knute Rockne

  Second All-American Team by United Press

- Professional Football:

Boston Redskins of the NFL for one year

Tulsa Oilers of the AFL for one year

QUOTE:

- Dr. James Naismith, the "Father of Basketball" is quoted as saying that Weller was "the most efficient dribbler" in the history of basketball up to that time.

- In a personal dedication by Frank W. McDonald former Haskell Athletic Director, to Louis Weller, he states: "Louie Rabbit Weller who has given me many, many thrills watching him 'cavort' on the gridiron. Your fabulous record as an athlete at the greatest of all Indian Schools.... has played an outstanding part in making Haskell famous."

1973 INDUCTION

ALBUQUERQUE, NEW MEXICO

Ellison Brown

ELLISON BROWN
Inducted 1973

DATE OF BIRTH: September 23, 1914

DATE OF DEATH: August 23, 1975

BIRTH PLACE: Westerly, Rhode Island

TRIBE: Narragansett

EDUCATION: Unknown

SPORTS DATA: Marathon

ACHIEVEMENTS:

- Member USA Olympic Marathon Team 1936

- Winner of Boston Marathon 1936

- Winner of Boston Marathon 1939

- First man in the world to break 2 ½ hours for the marathon race

COMMENTS:

Ellison Brown, a Narragansett Indian from Alton, Rhode Island, had been referred to as a self styled super human after completing one of the most sensational victory's in the history of Marathon racing. The year was 1939 and the bronzed skinned Indian had just cruised to a world's record in the 43rd running of the Boston marathon. He became the first runner in the world to break 2 ½ hours for such an endurance race.

Elmer Busch

ELMER BUSCH
Inducted 1973

DATE OF BIRTH: June 1, 1889

DATE OF DEATH: Unknown

BIRTH PLACE: California

TRIBE: Poma

EDUCATION: Carlisle

SPORTS DATA: Football: Tackle – Carlisle

ACHIEVEMENTS:

- 2nd team All-American Tackle 1913

- Captain Carlisle football team 1914

- All-Time Carlisle Indian team

COMMENTS:

- In 1911 Carlisle won 11 and lost 1 game.

- The team of 1912 averaged less than 170 lbs. with Busch who was 22 years old, the heaviest, weighing 186 pounds and standing 5'10" tall. In 14 games the Redskins piled up a total of 504 points as against their opponent's 114 points. Their record was 12 wins, 1 loss, and 1 tie.

- In 1913 Carlisle won 10, lost 1, and tied 1 game.

- The three center linemen Busch, Garlow and Hill consistently beat their heavier opponents, allowing the backs to plow through for good gains.

Albert Hawley

ALBERT M. HAWLEY
Inducted 1973

DATE OF BIRTH: March 13, 1906

DATE OF DEATH: April 2, 1999

BIRTH PLACE: Hays, Montana

TRIBE: Gos Ventre & Assiniboine

EDUCATION: Haskell Institute, Davis & Elkins College

SPORTS DATA: Football

ACHIEVEMENTS:

- All-State, All-Missouri Valley Center, All-Central Atlantic Conference

- Played in East-West Shrine Charity Football Game 1927

- Football All-American Honorable Mention 1928 and 1929

COMMENTS:

- "Hawley was Haskell's iron man; he went through the regular varsity season of eleven games and never missed a minute in any contest." Played regular center in 1925 – 1926 seasons. Elected captain of the team in 1927.

- On Coach R.E. Hanley's "All-Time, All-Haskell Indian Eleven".

- Enrolled at Davis & Elkins College fall 1928, and played varsity center position through 1931 and was team captain in 1930 and 1931.

- April 1966, received the Interior Department's Distinguished Service Award.

- Selected Outstanding Alumnus of Davis & Elkins College, August 1968.

- Selected Outstanding Alumnus for 1969 by Haskell Alumni Association.

- Nevada Amateur Athletic Union Boxing Commissioner

Frank Hudson

FRANK HUDSON
Inducted 1973

DATE OF BIRTH: June 6, 1875

DATE OF DEATH: June 1, 1959

BIRTH PLACE: Paguate, New Mexico

TRIBE: Laguna Pueblo

EDUCATION: Carlisle

SPORTS DATA: Football: Quarterback – Carlisle

ACHIEVEMENTS:

- Quarterback Second Team All-American 1890, Walter Camps Selection

- Captain Carlisle Football Team 1898

COMMENTS:

- "Hudson became one of the best players ever seen on any football field." His greatest asset was his ability to drop kick with unerring accuracy from 30 and 40 yards.

- Small in stature 5'6" and weighing only 130 lbs. he was a giant on the gridiron. He quarterbacked the team through three victories in one week, defeating Illinois 23-6, Cincinnati 10-0, and Ohio State 20-12.

- It was in the Penn game of 1897 that Frank Hudson established himself as the greatest drop kicker in the nation. It was an "unbelievable" game; Hudson kicked two perfect drop kicks to win a hard fought game. A week previous he defeated Yale by the same method.

- On December 27, 1896 Carlisle played and defeated Wisconsin, in what is known as the first game under electric light.

Walter Johnson

WALTER JOHNSON
Inducted 1973

DATE OF BIRTH: August 18, 1908

DATE OF DEATH: Unknown

BIRTH PLACE: In a cabin in the White Mountains on the
                   Nevada/California State Line

TRIBE: Paiute

EDUCATION: Haskell Institute and University of Redlands

SPORTS DATA: Football

ACHIEVEMENTS:

- Honorable mention All-American 1931 – fullback

- Annual East-West Shrine Football Game 1932 (West Team)

- All Kansas Honorable mention Fullback 1932

- All Conference Fullback University of Redlands 1934

COMMENTS:

- Quote – Sports Writer, Roy Cummings, January 1, 1932: "Punting honors seem to belong to Walter Johnson, the Haskell Indian Athlete. Johnson is an unorthodox kicker with very little form but he still has the prime requisite, he gets the ball down the field 50 yards every kick."

- In 1937 he began his 33 year career as teacher, advisor and coach at Sherman Indian School in Southern California. In 1948 he transferred to Stewart Indian School as a teacher and a coach until his retirement in 1970.

Wallace Little Finger

WALLACE LITTLE FINGER
Inducted 1973

DATE OF BIRTH: November 15, 1901

DATE OF DEATH: July 1, 1989

BIRTH PLACE: Pine Ridge Reservation, South Dakota

TRIBE: Sioux

EDUCATION: Haskell Institute

SPORTS DATA: Track and Field

ACHIEVEMENTS:

- Member of Haskell's 2-mile Relay Team 1926.

- Haskell's 2-mile Relay Team was one of the best 2-mile relay teams in the nation. The two-mile relay team was victorious at the Illinois, Kansas, Southwest and Drake relays, setting college division records and frequently competing in the University division and winning.

- During the mid-twenties Wallace Little Finger was consistently the power runner on Haskell Indian Schools two-mile and sprint-medley relay teams.

- Wallace Little Finger went by the name of Wallace Yellow Horse and would alternate between lead-off and anchorman on the two-mile relay, depending on the strength of their opponents.

Frank Mt. Pleasant

FRANK MT. PLEASANT
Inducted 1973

DATE OF BIRTH: January 8, 1883

DATE OF DEATH: July 1, 1971

BIRTH PLACE: Tuscarora Indian Reservation, New York

TRIBE: Tuscarora

EDUCATION: Carlisle

SPORTS DATA: Carlisle Football: Quarterback

                   Track & Field

ACHIEVEMENTS:

- Quarterback – All-Eastern Team 1905

  Second Team All-American 1905

  Honorable Mention All-American 1907

- Track & Field – United States Olympic Team 1908 Long Jump & Triple Jump

  Among Best 440 Dashmen in Nation 1908

COMMENTS:

- As he grew into manhood he became a man of many talents. Mt. Pleasant was an artist on the piano, a great lover of music. He was modest in conversation about athletics but through careful dedicated training he reached a rare state of perfection to become an athlete of world renown. It was said he could excel at any game requiring mental and physical strength.

- Quote: "To meet Frank is to like him. To know him is to admire him. To live in the same little world with him is to appreciate his sterling qualities and noble nature."

Bemus Pierce

BEMUS PIERCE
Inducted 1973

DATE OF BIRTH: February 28, 1873

DATE OF DEATH: February 15, 1957

BIRTH PLACE: Seneca Reservation, New York

TRIBE: Seneca

EDUCATION: Carlisle

SPORTS DATA: Football: Guard – Carlisle

ACHIEVEMENTS:

- Honorable Mention All-American Guard 1894

- Second Team All-American Guard 1896

- Captain Carlisle 1895, 1896, and 1897

- Professional Football Homestead Athletic Club 1900 – 1901

COMMENTS:

- Bemus Pierce became one of Carlisle's first All-Americans as a result of his ferocious playing at the line position. His six foot one and one-half inches, 225 pounds of muscle left vivid impressions on those who came in contact with him in football wars.

- In the years from 1894 to 1897 he reaped the plaudits of football coaches, sportswriters and the public for his prowess on the gridiron with the famous Indian teams of the time.

Cab Renick

JESSE B. "CAB" RENICK
Inducted 1973

DATE OF BIRTH: September 29, 1917

DATE OF DEATH: November 25, 1999

BIRTH PLACE: Love County, Marietta, Oklahoma

TRIBE: Choctaw

EDUCATION: Oklahoma A & M

SPORTS DATA: Basketball: Forward

ACHIEVEMENTS:

- Helms foundation All American 1939 & 1940

- NEA All American 1939 & 1940

- AAU All American 1947 & 1948

- Captain 1948 USA Olympic Basketball Team

- Gold Medal Winner – USA Basketball Team Olympic Games 1948

COMMENTS:

- Upon graduating from college Renick was commissioned an officer in the US Navy and received his wings as a Naval Pilot.

- After his military service, he played basketball for the Phillips 66 Oilers and in 1948 was selected to the USA Olympic Basketball Team. He was chosen Captain of the team and was carried off the floor by his teammates following their 65 – 21 victory over France to capture the Olympic Basketball Championship.

- In 1948 Jesse "Cab" Renick became coach; player of the Phillips 66 team and in his first 3 seasons won 153 games and lost only 9 for a winning percentage of .944.

- In 1961 Renick experienced one of his greatest moments when he adopted and became the father of six orphaned Indian children.

Ed Rogers

ED ROGERS
Inducted 1973

DATE OF BIRTH: April 14, 1876

DATE OF DEATH: October 16, 1971

BIRTH PLACE: Libby, Minnesota

TRIBE: White Earth Chippewa

EDUCATION: Carlisle & University of Minnesota

SPORTS DATA: Football: End – Carlisle & University of Minnesota

ACHIEVEMENTS:

- 1903 Third Team All-American Walter Camps Selection

- Among the University of Minnesota's most famous captains – Captain 1901

- Enshrined in Footballs Hall of Fame for Pioneer College Players.

COMMENTS:

- Rogers was a key factor in the history making Minnesota tie Michigan game in 1903. It was from this game the "Little Brown Jug" tradition was started.

- Upon leaving Minnesota in 1904 he returned to Carlisle as football coach for one year. His team won 9, lost 2 and was rated 14th in the country.

- The remarkable Rogers practiced law for 62 years. In 1963 he was named the Outstanding Country Attorney in the United States. He retired in 1966 at the age of 90.

Angelita Rosal

ANGELITA ROSAL
Inducted 1973

DATE OF BIRTH: March 28, 1956

BIRTH PLACE: San Francisco, California

TRIBE: Sioux

EDUCATION: Unknown

SPORTS DATA: Table Tennis

ACHIEVEMENTS:

- Competed in World Junior Table Tennis Championship. England 1966

- Toured the U.S. as member of the U.S. Women's Team competing against the Peoples Republic of China. 1967

- Tied for 1st Place in USA finals for World Championships. 1972

- Competed in the World Table Tennis Championships at Savajevo, Yugoslavia. Represented the USA in singles, mixed and women's doubles. 1973

- 1976, US Closed finalist.

- 1982, National Sports Festival, wins singles.

- 1982, Harvard Open, singles finalist and wins Mixed.

- Inducted into the USATT Hall of Fame in 1996.

COMMENTS:

- Angelita is a very talented young lady and at the age of 17 is a remarkably accomplished athlete. She is of Sioux and Filipino ancestry, and justly proud of both.

- Angelita began playing table tennis at the age of nine and achieved such incredible proficiency that at 12 she became US Singles Champion for girls under 13.

- After winning a number of national titles, in 1973 she qualified to compete in the World Championships in Sarajevo, Yugoslavia.

Gustavus Welch

GUSTAVUS "GUS" WELCH
Inducted 1973

DATE OF BIRTH: December 23, 1892

DATE OF DEATH: January 28, 1970

BIRTH PLACE: Spooner, Wisconsin

TRIBE: Chippewa

EDUCATION: Carlisle

SPORTS DATA: Football: Quarterback

ACHIEVEMENTS:

- Second Team All-American Quarterback 1913

- Captain of Carlisle Football Team 1913

- Professional Football, Canton Ohio Bulldogs 1915 – 1917

COMMENTS:

- Welch attended Carlisle and played on their football team during the Indian School's height of excellence in sports – 1911, 1912 and 1913. During these years Carlisle won 33, tied 2, and lost 3 games. Carlisle was the only school in the nation who would week after week play the top teams in the nation. He could do anything any coach could expect of a dream quarterback.

- Gus Welch, 5'11", 152 lbs., Chippewa from Minnesota, and Captain of the 1913 Team was ranked as one of the three best quarterbacks in the nation. Was named Second Team All-American 1913 as well as Honorable Mention on many Sports Writers lists.

Jimmie Wolfe

JIMMIE WOLF, JR.
Inducted 1973

DATE OF BIRTH: December 28, 1934

BIRTH PLACE: Mountain View, Oklahoma

TRIBE: Kiowa

EDUCATION: Panhandle A&M State College

SPORTS DATA: Football

ACHIEVEMENTS:

- 3rd Team All-American NAIA 1958

- 3rd Team Associated Press Little All-American 1958

COMMENTS:

- Jr. Wolf set the National Small College Season Scoring Record of 25 touchdowns in 1958.

- Wolf set the National Small College Single Game Scoring Record of 8 touchdowns in 1958.

- National College Division Scoring Champion 1958.

QUOTE: Kansas City UPI

- "Jr. Wolf, Kiowa Indian playing halfback for Panhandle A&M of Goodwell, Oklahoma, went on the warpath with 8 touchdowns last weekend beating the single game scoring records of the National Association of Intercollegiate Athletics."

1977 INDUCTION

LAWRENCE, KANSAS

Chester Ellis

CHESTER L. "CHET" ELLIS
Inducted 1977

DATE OF BIRTH: August 27, 1913

DATE OF DEATH: January 16, 1986

BIRTH PLACE: Red House, New York

TRIBE: Seneca

EDUCATION: Haskell Institute

SPORTS DATA: Boxing – Amateur and Professional

ACHIEVEMENTS:

- Kansas National Guard Camp Champion, 126 pound division, as member of Troop "I" 114th Cavalry, Kansas National Guard, Haskell Institute, Lawrence, Kansas – 1935 and 1936.

- Featherweight Champion, AAU, Haskell Institute, 1935-1937

- Captain of Haskell Boxing Team, 1935 – 1937.

- Kansas City Star Golden Gloves Bantamweight Champion, 1938 and 1939.

- National Golden Gloves Bantamweight Champion 1939.

- International golden Gloves Bantamweight 1939.

QUOTE – Kansas City Star:

> "As a member of the 1939 Kansas City Star Team, Chester Ellis was the first Indian to win a national title in Golden Gloves competition. When he fought his way to the international bantamweight boxing championship, he became the first member of his fighting race ever to achieve the supreme crown in the sport. Kansas City is proud of its champion. He is a 100 percent American, both by blood and by spirit."

Stacy Howell

STACY S. HOWELL
Inducted 1977

DATE OF BIRTH: January 28, 1928

DATE OF DEATH: March 11, 1997

BIRTH PLACE: Maryville, Missouri

TRIBE: Pawnee

EDUCATION: Pawnee High School; Pawnee, Oklahoma

Murray Junior College; Tishomingo, Oklahoma

Idaho University; Moscow, Idaho

East Central College; Ada, Oklahoma

SPORTS DATA: Basketball

ACHIEVEMENTS:

- Stacy was a four-year letterman at Pawnee, Oklahoma in basketball, football, and track, making the All-State Team in 1946 in football and basketball. He attended Murray A&M Junior College in 1947 and 1948, and was a selection for All-Conference honors both years and in 1948 he was a Junior College All-American. Howell lettered at Idaho University in

1949. Coming to East Central as a senior in 1949, Stacy was the number two scorer on the squad with 403 points, and was chosen as a member of the All-Conference second team. In the Oklahoma AAU tournament, Stacy amazed the onlookers with his unusual dribbling ability and flawless floor work. This excellent performance coupled with his unorthodox and accurate shots, won him NAIB All-American honors in 1950 and the Helm Foundation All-American selection.

QUOTE: Kansas City Star

"Howell is the most popular player in the NAIB tournament. He thrilled the crowd with his game winning goal the first night and continued with his flashy style of play to win more attention and ovations than any other individual in the tournament."

Jack Jacobs

JACK JACOBS
Inducted 1977

DATE OF BIRTH: August 7, 1919

DATE OF DEATH: January 12, 1974

BIRTH PLACE: Holdenville, Oklahoma

TRIBE: Creek

EDUCATION: Oklahoma University, Norman, Oklahoma

SPORTS DATA: Football

ACHIEVEMENTS:

- Muskogee High School football, 1932-1937

- Quarterback Selection on the All-State Team, 1936

- Outstanding player in the first Oklahoma Prep All-Star game, 1937

- Started at Quarterback for Oklahoma University, 1939-1941

- Established kicking record for Oklahoma University, 47.8 yard average, 1939

- Played in East – West Shrine Game, 1942

- College All-Star Game, 1942

- Played with Cleveland Rams,1942

- Played with Washington Redskins, 1945

- Played with Green bay Packers,1946

- Played with Winnipeg Blue Bombers, 1950-1955

- Led Bombers to the Grey Cup finals, 1950 & 1953

COMMENTS:

- Played 22 years without missing a season.

- Played Service baseball with Joe DiMaggio

- Played professional Baseball in 1948

- He excelled in baseball, football and basketball

- He was amateur golf champion of Manitoba

- Enshrined in the Canadian National League Hall of Fame in 1973

Clyde James

CLYDE L. "CHIEF" JAMES
Inducted 1977

DATE OF BIRTH: March 9, 1900

DATE OF DEATH: June 13, 1982

BIRTH PLACE: Oklahoma Indian Territory

TRIBE: Modoc

EDUCATION: Seneca High School, Seneca, Missouri

                   Southwest Missouri State College, Springfield, Missouri

SPORTS DATA: Basketball

ACHIEVEMENTS:

- Earned varsity letter in basketball at Southwest Missouri State College, 1921-1924

- Played forward on SWSC basketball team which won Missouri Inter-Collegiate Association Championship title – setting scoring record – elected Captain of All-League Team, 1924

- Led Missouri Valley AAU in scoring field goals, 1924

- Selected as Tournament All-Star forward of Tri-State District Basketball champions – Barnsdall B Squares of Seneca, Missouri, 1924

- Played with Tulsa Eagles, Tulsa Diamond Oilers, AAU Basketball Teams – rated as one of the greatest forwards in amateur basketball. In 1929 led Missouri Valley AAU in scoring field goals and played on two teams winning national championship titles during his career, 1924-1947.

QUOTE:

- William "Little Bill" Miller, Coach, NAAU Champions

"This lithe Indian lad, "Chief" James, became one of the legendary heroes of Missouri basketball, compiling amazing scoring records with Andy McDonald's fine Springfield Teachers' College teams. He subsequently led the Missouri Valley AAU League – Which has furnished the last eight national amateur champions – in scoring one season."

Rollie Munsell

ROLLIE THURMAN MUNSELL, JR.
Known as "June" or Junior Munsell
Inducted 1977

DATE OF BIRTH: May 30, 1913

DATE OF DEATH: April 29, 1996

BIRTH PLACE: Tuttle, Oklahoma

TRIBE: Chickasaw

EDUCATION: Chilocco Indian School, Chilocco,
                    Oklahoma

SPORTS DATA: Boxing – Amateur/Professional

ACHIEVEMENTS:

- Chilocco boxing team for four years earned the following titles:

  Missouri Valley AAU Championship, 160 pound division 1932

  Missouri Valley AAU Championship, 160 pound division 1933

Missouri Valley AAU Championship, 175 pound division
1934

Missouri Valley AAU Championship, heavyweight division
1935

Professional:

- Professional boxer 1936-1942 fought over 100 fights from coast to coast in the Heavyweight class. Fought such boxers as Babe Hunt, Max Baer, and other leading world heavyweight contenders before going into the US Marines in World War II, where he served as boxing instructor.

- October 4, 1938 won Indian Heavyweight Boxing Championship of the World Belt. This championship title recognized by the National Boxing Association, and the belt awarded by Ring Magazine and personally presented by Nat Fleisher, Ring editor.

- August 7, 1976, Enshrined in the Oklahoma Athletic Hall of Fame.

Phillip Osif

PHILLIP OSIF
Inducted 1977

DATE OF BIRTH: 1906 – Exact date unknown

DATE OF DEATH: September 1, 1956

BIRTH PLACE: Pima Indian Reservation, Sacaton, Arizona

TRIBE: Pima

EDUCATION: Haskell Institute, Lawrence, Kansas

SPORTS DATA: Track and Cross Country

ACHIEVEMENTS:

- Captain, 1927 Haskell Cross Country Team

- Captain, 1927 Haskell Track Team

- Member of 1927 Haskell 2-mile relay Team – undefeated in Texas Relays, Kansas Relays, Knights of Columbus Games, Penn Relay Games, and Rice Relays

- National AAU Junior and Senior 6-mile champion

- 1500-meter Illinois Relay Champion

- 3000-meter Kansas University Relay Champion

- Missouri Valley AAU 2-mile record holder 1927

QUOTE: 1927 Haskell Annual

"Haskell's indoor track season came to a successful close when Coach Dick Hanley entered his star, Captain Osif, in a two-mile special event against a relay of Kansas and Missouri freshmen at the annual Kansas University-Missouri dual meet held at Convention Hall. A Kansas and a Missouri freshman took Osif through the first mile and turned over a twenty-yard lead to a lone Kansas University freshman who increased the lead given to him to fifty yards in the first half of the last mile. From this mark Osif began to cut down his opponent's lead on the last lap caught his rival and raced his rival's heart out in the last seventy yards, winning with ten yards to spare and breaking the Missouri Valley record, setting a new mark of 9 minutes 28 3/10ths seconds."

1978 INDUCTION

LAWRENCE, KANSAS

Harold Foster

HAROLD "CHUCK" FOSTER, JR.

Inducted 1978

DATE OF BIRTH: May 2, 1952

BIRTH PLACE: Fort Defiance, Arizona

TRIBE: Navajo

EDUCATION: Central Arizona College, Coolidge, Arizona

SPORTS DATA: Track and Cross Country

ACHIEVEMENTS:

- Varsity Track letterman, Central Arizona College, 1971-1973

- Varsity Cross-Country letterman, Central Arizona College, 1971-1973

- Arizona Community College Athletic Conference Champion for 3-mile, 1972-1973

- Arizona Community College Athletic Conference Champion for 1-mile, 1973

- Arizona Community College Athletic Conference Cross-Country Champion, 1971- 1972 finishing 5th and 3rd in the nation

- Named to second team position on the All-American Cross-Country of the NJCAA for the year 1971

- Named to first team position on the All-American Cross-Country of the NJCAA for the year 1972

- Central Arizona College record holder in 880 yard, 1- mile, 2-mile, and 3-mile events with the fastest time in the nation for a Junior College in 1973

QUOTE:

- George Young, Track Coach –

"While attending school, he was the Arizona Community College Athletic conference Cross Country Champion in 1971 and 1972, finishing 5th and 3rd in the nation. This earned him All-American honors for both years."

William Mills

WILLIAM "BILLY" MILLS
Inducted 1978

DATE OF BIRTH: June 30, 1938

BIRTH PLACE: Pine Ridge, South Dakota

TRIBE: Oglala Lakota "Sioux"

EDUCATION: Haskell Indian School, Lawrence, Kansas

                   University of Kansas, Lawrence, Kansas

SPORTS DATA: Track and Cross Country

ACHIEVEMENTS:

- Kansas University 1957-1962

    1st Team NCAA Cross Country All-American 1958

    2nd Team NCAA Cross Country All-American 1959

    National AAU Cross Country All-American 1959

    1st Team NCAA Cross Country All-American 1960

    Member of Kansas University's NCAA Championship Track and Field Team 1960

- Gold medal Olympic 10,000 meter run, Tokyo, Japan, 1964

- Olympic Marathon, Tokyo, Japan 1964

- National AAU All-American Track and Field and Cross Country, 1964

- World record 6 mile run, US National Track and Field Championships, San Diego, California, 1965

- American record 3 mile US National Indoor Championships, New York, NY, 1965

- American record 3,000 meter indoors, London, England, 1965

- American record 10,000 meter, Augsburg, Germany, 1965

- National AAU All-American Track and Field, 1965

- Inducted into the National Track and Field Hall of Fame, the USA Olympic Hall of Fame and the World Sports Humanitarian Hall of Fame.

COMMENTS:

- Billy contributes his success as an athlete and individual to the values of character, dignity and pride instilled in him by his coaches at Haskell and later throughout his career, especially Tony Coffin from Haskell, Bill Easton from Kansas University, and Tommy Thompson, Sr. from the US Naval Academy and USMC.

QUOTE:

- Avery Brundage, former President of the International Olympic Committee. "I have been watching the Olympic Games for over 50 years and have never seen an American respond greater to pressure than Billy did in winning the Olympic 10,000 m."

Joseph Sahmaunt

JOSEPH H. "BUD" SAHMAUNT
Inducted 1978

DATE OF BIRTH: November 5, 1938

BIRTH PLACE: Lawton, Oklahoma

TRIBE: Kiowa

EDUCATION: Cameron State Junior College, Lawton, Oklahoma

                   Oklahoma City University, Oklahoma City, Oklahoma

                   Southwestern State University, Weatherford, Oklahoma

                   University of Minnesota, Minneapolis, Minnesota

SPORTS DATA: Basketball

ACHIEVEMENTS:

- Varsity Basketball letterman, Cameron State Junior College 1956-1958

- All-Conference Team, Oklahoma Junior College Conference 1956-1957

- All-Tournament Team, Arkansas City Junior College Invitational, Arkansas City, Kansas 1956-1957

- All-Conference Team, Pioneer Junior College Conference, 1957-1958

- Outstanding Basketball Player Award, Cameron State Junior College, 1957-1958

- Most Valuable Player, All-States Jaycees Classic Tournament, 1957-1958

- All-American Second Team position, All-American Basketball Squad of the NJCAA for the year 1957-1958

- Varsity Basketball letterman, Oklahoma City University two years 1958-1960

- Most Valuable Player, All-College Tournament, Oklahoma City, Oklahoma 1958- 1959

- All-Tournament Team, All-College Tournament, Oklahoma City, Oklahoma two years 1958-1960

- All-American Honorable Mention, Associated Press 1959-1960

- Daily Oklahoman, All-decade Basketball Team 1950's – 1975

- Athletic Director at Oklahoma City University, 1987-2000

QUOTE:

- Oklahoma City AP

"Bud Sahmaunt, Oklahoma City's little 5-9 full-blood Kiowa Indian from Elgin, was named the tournament's outstanding player by sportswriters, coaches, and officials."

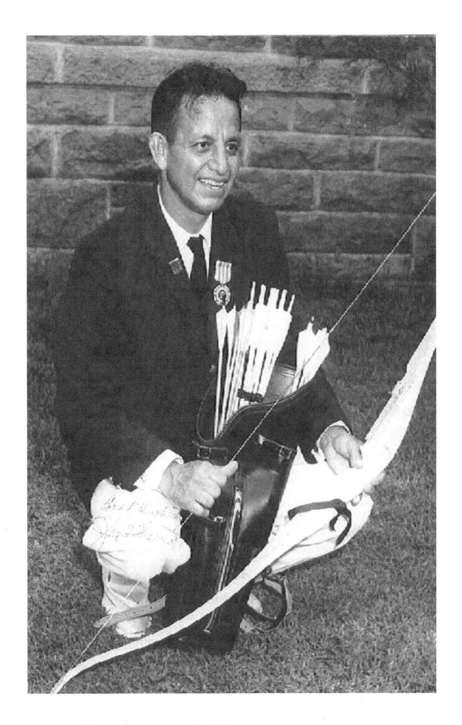

Joe Thornton

JOE TINDLE THORNTON
Inducted 1978

DATE OF BIRTH: August 2, 1916

BIRTH PLACE: Stilwell, Oklahoma

TRIBE: Cherokee

EDUCATION: Chilocco Indian School

SPORTS DATA: Archery

ACHIEVEMENTS:

- 1961 Archery World Champion (set 3 world records), Oslo, Norway

- 1962 Won British International Trials Archery Championship, Windsor, England

- 1963 Second Place, World Championship Archery Tournament, Helsinki, Finland

- 1965 Second place, World Championship Archery Tournament, Vasteras, Sweden

- 1967 Member of U.S. Archery Team that competed in World Tournament in Amersfoort, Holland (team won world team championship)

- 1970 National Archer Champion, Oxford, Ohio

- 1971Member of U.S. Archery Team that competed in World Archery Tournament in York, England (team won world team championship)

SPECIAL RECOGNITION:

- 1962 Selected by Council of American Indians as most Distinguished American Indian and presented key to City of Tulsa.

- 1964 Selected for the book, "Who's Who in Oklahoma". Appeared on CBS Television programs, "What's My Line" and "Heywood Hale Brown Sports Interviews"

- 1968 Elected to three-year term as Member of Board of Governors of National Archery Association

- 1972 Elected President of Oklahoma State Archery Association

Egbert Ward

EGBERT BRYAN "EG" WARD
Inducted 1978

DATE OF BIRTH: October 18, 1900

DATE OF DEATH: April 2, 1994

BIRTH PLACE: Toppenish, Washington

TRIBE: Yakima

EDUCATION: Washington   State   College,   Pullman,
                   Washington

                   Haskell Institute, Lawrence, Kansas

SPORTS DATA: Football, Baseball and Basketball

ACHIEVEMENTS:

- Varsity four-year football letterman, Haskell Institute, Lawrence, Kansas, 1923, 1924, 1925 and 1926. Varsity baseball letterman, Haskell Institute, Lawrence, Kansas, 1924, 1925 and 1926. Captain Haskell Baseball Team 1926. Varsity Basketball letterman, Haskell Institute, Lawrence, Kansas, 1925, 1926 and 1927. Named to Kansas All-State Backfield, 1926. Named Haskell's Greatest Quarterback and selected as Quarterback on All-Time All-Haskell Indian Eleven, 1926, by Coach Richard "Dick" Hanley.

QUOTE: 1927 Haskell Annual

- "The football season of 1926 was unquestionably the most significant in the history of Haskell's gridiron competition, if not, indeed, in the whole history of the Indian race. It saw at Haskell the dedication of the first and only Indian stadium and at the same time brought forth the strongest eleven which ever brought glory and fame to the Purple and Gold".

1980 INDUCTION

LAWRENCE, KANSAS

Robert Gawboy

ROBERT "BOB" GAWBOY
Inducted 1980

DATE OF BIRTH: June 28, 1932

DATE OF DEATH: July 15, 1987

BIRTH PLACE: Vermillion   Lake   Indian   Reservation,
                    Minnesota

TRIBE: Chippewa

EDUCATION: Purdue University

SPORTS DATA: Aquatics – Swimming

ACHIEVEMENTS:

- 1st place winner, 150 yard Individual Medley, 1950 Collegiate East-West Meet, Ft. Lauderdale, Florida

- 2nd place winner, 150 yard Individual Medley, 1952 NCAA Championships Meet

- Gold Medal Winner, 220 yard breaststroke, at Indoor National AAU Aquatic Meet at Yale University, on April 1, 1955, with World Record time of 2:38.0

QUOTE: Minnesota Swimmer

"Gawboy started working out again in February, 1955. On April 1, 1955, he swam his first race in over two years – the 220 yard breast (underwater breast allowed) at the Indoor National AAU's at Yale University. T'was unbelievable, but Bob cracked the American Record in the prelims, and in the finals won the gold medal with a World Record Time of 2:38.0 (at that time short course world records were recognized). Remarkable, as he had not swam a race for over two years, he had just undergone surgery, and he had been in training for less than three months."

Elijah Smith

ELIJAH "ELI" SMITH
Inducted 1980

DATE OF BIRTH: May 3, 1902

DATE OF DEATH: October 12, 1998

BIRTH PLACE: Oneida, Wisconsin

TRIBE: Oneida

EDUCATION: Haskell Institute, Lawrence, Kansas

                   Davis & Elkins College, Elkins, West Virginia

SPORTS DATA: Football, Baseball and Track

ACHIEVEMENTS:

- Member of team awarded a special gold football with a cut diamond representing Undefeated and Highest Scoring Team in the Nation – The Haskell Indians, of 1926.

- Haskell Institute – 1923-1926

- Varsity four-year football letterman, 1923-1926.

- Varsity four-year baseball letterman, 1923-1926

- Varsity three-year track letterman, 1923-1925

- Captain, 1925 Haskell Indians Baseball Team and holder of special record "Batting Average" for one season of .650 percent.

- In 1926 named to Kansas All-State College backfield Second Team and to Halfback on All-Time All-Haskell Indian Second Team.

- Holder of special record at Haskell Institute for most points after touchdown as a place kicker.

- Named on "All Opponent" Team selected by Boston College in 1926, and his 75- yard run for touchdown against Bucknell University on the day the new Haskell Stadium was dedicated was given recognition by Helms Athletic Foundation as one of the "best" of the 1926 season.

- Davis & Elkins College – 1928-1930

- Varsity football and varsity baseball letterman – voted best ball carrier and place kicker on State Championship Team in West Virginia in 1929.

QUOTE:

- Haskell Annual – "Eli Smith, Haskell's fastest back, came into his own in the 1926 season. Even at Haskell where good backs have been abundant in times past it is seldom that one of Eli's caliber has been developed and it is extremely doubtful if his 1926 performance has ever been surpassed. His long, dazzling runs this year brought the stands to their feet in many cities throughout the United States, Boston, Bucknell, Michigan State, in fact, all the teams encountered this season will testify to his speed and drive."

Martin Wheelock

MARTIN FREDERICK WHEELOCK

Inducted 1980

DATE OF BIRTH: 1874

DATE OF DEATH: May 25, 1937

BIRTH PLACE: Oneida, Wisconsin

TRIBE: Oneida

EDUCATION: Carlisle Indian School, Carlisle, Pennsylvania

SPORTS DATA: Football

ACHIEVEMENTS:

- Varsity Football letterman at Carlisle Indian School 1894-1902

- Captain Carlisle Football Team 1899

- Selected by sports Department, Philadelphia Inquirer for All-University Team, 1902

- National honor selection to All-American Second Team, 1901

QUOTE: Fabulous Redmen

- "Coach Warner was once asked by a Carlisle Herald reporter to name an All-Time Carlisle Indian Team. According to the reporter, this was Warner's choice for the position of tackle: Emile (Wauseka) Houser, Martin Wheelock. Warner explained his selections by estimating the merits of each man. Wauseka and Wheelock …. Used their brains to advantage."

1981 INDUCTION

LAWRENCE, KANSAS

David Bray

DAVID W. BRAY
Inducted 1981

DATE OF BIRTH: May 19, 1955

BIRTH PLACE: Gowanda, New York

TRIBE: Seneca

EDUCATION: Cornell University

SPORTS DATA: Lacrosse, Track/Cross Country, Basketball

ACHIEVEMENTS:

- 1973 Most Valuable Track Man – Gowanda Central School

- 1973 Sportsmanship Award, Newton Lacrosse Club

- 1974 Most Valuable Player Award, Newton Lacrosse Club

- 1972-73-74 North American Lacrosse Association All-Star

- 1975-76-77 Varsity Lacrosse, Cornell University

- 1976 Most Valuable Player – Seneca Nation of Indians Basketball Tournament

- 1977 North/South All-Star Game

- Honorable Mention All-American

- American Indian Athletic Award

Nelson Levering

NELSON B. LEVERING
Inducted 1981

DATE OF BIRTH: September 20, 1926

DATE OF DEATH: February 28, 2005

BIRTH PLACE: Macy, Nebraska

TRIBE: Omaha/Bannock

EDUCATION: Haskell Institute

SPORTS DATA: Boxing

ACHIEVEMENTS:

- Midwest Golden Gloves champion, 147 pound Division, 1947

- Kansas State Welterweight Champion. Fought 40 Amateur bouts with 35 Wins – 5 Losses, 1948

- Professional "Prospect of Month" – Lightweight Division Record Reflects 50 Professional Fights with 23 Wins – 17 K.O.'s – 5 Losses, 1949

COMMENTS:

- Fought on boxing Card with Joe Louis four (4) times while Louis was heavyweight champion of the World.

- Member of boxing Stable of "Rocky Marciano"

Austin Tincup

AUSTIN BEN TINCUP
Inducted 1981

DATE OF BIRTH: April 14, 1892

DATE OF DEATH: July 5, 1980

BIRTH PLACE: Rogers County, Oklahoma

TRIBE: Cherokee

EDUCATION: Elementary School

SPORTS DATA: Baseball

ACHIEVEMENTS:

- Major League Baseball: Pitcher

- Philadelphia Phillies, 1914, 1915, 1916, 1918

- Chicago Cubs, 1928

- Won recognition as a pitching coach and scout with the Yankees, Pirates, Browns, and Phillies.

- Inducted into the Oklahoma Baseball Hall of Fame in 1971

1982 INDUCTION

LAWRENCE, KANSAS

Amos Aitson

AMOS AITSON
Inducted 1982

DATE OF BIRTH: October 18, 1928

DATE OF DEATH: October 10, 2003

BIRTH PLACE: Carnegie, Oklahoma

TRIBE: Kiowa

EDUCATION: Riverside Indian School, Anadarko, Oklahoma

SPORTS DATA: Football and Boxing

ACHIEVEMENTS:

- Football letterman, Riverside Indian School 1944

- Boxing letterman, Riverside Indian School 1945

- As member of Riverside Indian School Boxing Team was runner up for Oklahoma Golden Gloves Bantamweight Title 1944, 1945

- Winner of 57th Annual National AAU Boxing Championships, 118 pound class, at Boston Garden, North Station, Boston, Massachusetts, April 3, 1945

QUOTE:

- 1946 Britannica Book of the Year (p. 137)

  "Boxers from New Orleans, Louisiana; Oklahoma City, Oklahoma; Philadelphia; Chicago; Buffalo; Alexandria, Virginia and Cleveland were returned champions. A feature of the tournament was the success of two Indian participants Amos Aitson and Virgil Franklin, members of the Oklahoma City team, who won the bantamweight and featherweight championships, respectively."

George Levi

GEORGE "LITTLE SKEE" LEVI
Inducted 1982

DATE OF BIRTH: November 10, 1899

DATE OF DEATH: September 16, 1988

BIRTH PLACE: Bridgeport, Oklahoma

TRIBE: Arapaho

EDUCATION: Haskell Institute, Lawrence, Kansas 1922

                 Phillips University

SPORTS DATA: Football

ACHIEVEMENTS:

- Haskell Institute – played football, basketball and ran track from 1922-1926

- Captain of football team 1925

- Played on the 1926 undefeated Haskell football team

- All-American Honorable mention

- All-Time, All-Haskell second team

- Inducted into the Kansas Sports Hall of Fame 1981

Thomas Yarr

THOMAS CORNELIUS YARR
"WAHOO"
Inducted 1982

DATE OF BIRTH: December 4, 1908

DATE OF DEATH: December 24, 1941

BIRTH PLACE: Chimacum, Washington

TRIBE: Snohomish

EDUCATION: Notre Dame University, South Bend, Indiana

SPORTS DATA: Football

ACHIEVEMENTS:

- Notre Dame University Varsity three year letterman, 1929-1931

- Played center on Knute Rockne's last "Fighting Irish" National Championship Team 1930

- Captain, Notre Dame Football Team 1931

- Named All-American Center on Associated Press Consensus Team and many others 1931

- Member Notre Dame Athletic Hall of Fame

QUOTE: Press Box

- Notre Dame Coach Frank Leahy commented, "Tom Yarr came up the hard way at Notre Dame. He came from a little town in the State of Washington with no reputation, but he fought his way to the top by his willingness to trade a lot of hard effort for success. All American Center in 1931, he easily rates as one of the best centers in Notre Dame history."

1985 INDUCTION

LAWRENCE, KANSAS

Sampson Bird

SAMPSON GEORGE "SAM" BIRD
Inducted 1985

DATE OF BIRTH: August 14, 1885

DATE OF DEATH: January 24, 1952

BIRTH PLACE: Browning, Montana

TRIBE: Blackfeet

EDUCATION: Carlisle Indian School, Carlisle, Pennsylvania

SPORTS DATA: Football/ Lacrosse/ Track and Field

ACHIEVEMENTS:

- Varsity Football letterman at Carlisle Indian School 1909, 1910, 1911, 1914, 1915

- Captain, Carlisle Indians Football Team 1911

- All-American Honorable Mention 1911

- Lacrosse Letterman at Carlisle Indian School 1909, 1910, 1911

- Captain, Carlisle Indians Lacrosse Team 1910

- Track and Field Letterman at Carlisle Indian School 1909, 1910, 1911

QUOTE:

- Browning Chief Newspaper

  "Loved and respected by his neighbors and friends of all creeds, Indian and white, his loss will be felt by all."

Virgil Franklin

VIRGIL R. FRANKLIN
Inducted 1985

DATE OF BIRTH: April 10, 1928

DATE OF DEATH: January 5, 1998

BIRTH PLACE: Lawton, Oklahoma

TRIBE: Arapaho/Kiowa

EDUCATION: Riverside Indian School, Anadarko, Oklahoma

                   Chilocco Indian School, Oklahoma

                   Murray State College, Tishomingo, Oklahoma

SPORTS DATA: Boxing/Football/Baseball/Track

ACHIEVEMENTS:

- In 118 pound class, winner of Southwest Oklahoma Golden Gloves and Oklahoma State AAU Boxing Tournament Titles and Semifinalist in 56th Annual National AAU Championships tournament, Boston, Massachusetts – 1944

- In 126 pound class, winner of Southwest Oklahoma Golden Gloves, Oklahoma State Golden Gloves, and Oklahoma State AAU Boxing Tournament titles – 1945

- Winner of National Golden Gloves Championship, 126 pound class, Chicago Tournament of Champions, Chicago, Illinois, March 10, 1945

- Winner of 57th Annual National AAU Boxing Championships Tournament, 126 pound class, held at Boston, Massachusetts, April 3, 1945

- In US Navy – winner of Featherweight Division Southwest Pacific Title in Marianas Island and All Armed Forces Title in Philippine Islands – 1946

- Chilocco Indian School – Winner All Indian Boxing Tourney, Muskogee, Oklahoma; Delta Bowl Events, Memphis, Tennessee; Mayor's Christmas Tree Fund, Wichita, Kansas; and Oklahoma State AAU Boxing Tournament Championship, Anadarko, Oklahoma – 1947

- Murray State College – Winner Tri-State Boxing Tourney, St. Louis, Missouri, and Oklahoma State AAU Boxing Tournament Championship, Ardmore, Oklahoma – 1948

- Excelled in Boxing – Four-sport letterman at all three schools he attended

QUOTE:

The Daily Oklahoman "Mighty Feather is big inspiration to Gloves mates."

Robert Holmes

ROBERT "BOBBY" HOLMES
Inducted 1985

DATE OF BIRTH: November 4, 1911

DATE OF DEATH: April 16, 2003

BIRTH PLACE: Miami, Oklahoma

TRIBE: Ottawa

EDUCATION: Haskell Institute, Lawrence, Kansas

                    Riverside Junior College, Riverside, California

                    Texas Technological College, Lubbock, Texas

SPORTS DATA: Football, Track and Field

ACHIEVEMENTS:

- Haskell Institute: Varsity Football Letterman 1931-34, Varsity Track and Field Letterman 1930-34. In 1932 Holmes ran 100 yard dash in 9.6 seconds in dual meet with Kansas University and threw Javelin 186 feet, eight inches in meet with Emporia State College and Baker University, establishing new Haskell High School Record, 1929-1934

- Riverside Junior College: Varsity Football Letterman 1936, Varsity Track and Field Letterman 1937

- Texas Technological College: Varsity Football Letterman 1937-38, Varsity Track and Field Letterman 1938-40, Halfback on Texas Tech Red Raiders Conference Championship Football Team Played in Sun Bowl Game January 1, 1938, Halfback on Texas Tech Red Raiders Conference Championship Football Team played in Cotton Bowl Game January 1, 1939, Signed contract and made Training Camp Cut for Halfback on Brooklyn Dodgers Professional Football Team, 1937-1940.

COMMENTS: Quote: The Daily Oklahoman

"Ottawa star is sensation in open field."

Gordon House

"CHIEF" GORDON A. HOUSE
Inducted 1985

DATE OF BIRTH: December 28, 1925

DATE OF DEATH: April 5, 1950

BIRTH PLACE: Fort Defiance, Arizona

TRIBE: Navajo/Oneida

EDUCATION: Phoenix Indian School, Phoenix, Arizona

Fort Wingate Indian School, Fort Wingate, New Mexico, Albuquerque Indian School, Albuquerque, New Mexico

SPORTS DATA: Boxing – Amateur/Professional

ACHIEVEMENTS:

- Golden Gloves amateur competition in Arizona and New Mexico 1940-1942

- Military Service amateur competition in California and the Hawaiian Islands as member of 2nd U.S. Marine Division 1943-1945

- April 19, 1945 won All Service Lightweight Division Boxing Championship – Pacific Ocean and Hawaiian Islands Area

- Professional Boxer 1946-1949

- Nat Fleischer's Ring Record Book Credits:

  July 25, 1948 – Arizona State Lightweight Title and Ring Belt

  August 23, 1948 – Nevada State Lightweight Title and Ring Belt

  October 20, 1948 – Texas State Lightweight Title and Ring Belt

  July 15, 1949 – Sandy Sadler, New York, New York KO by 5 (Sadler ranked in Ring Magazine, Featherweight Champion of the World – enshrined in "World Hall of Fame")

QUOTE:

- The Ringsider, boxing publication

  "Lightweight with a heavyweight punch"

- Knockout Magazine

  "Knockout Artist"

1987 INDUCTION

LAWRENCE, KANSAS

Arthur Bensell

ARTHUR S. BENSELL
Inducted 1987

DATE OF BIRTH: April 23, 1909

BIRTH PLACE: Siletz, Oregon

TRIBE: Mackanutunne (Siletz)

EDUCATION: Heidelberg College, Tiffin, Ohio

Bowling State University, Bowling Green, Ohio

SPORTS DATA: Football

ACHIEVEMENTS:

- Heidelberg Varsity Football Letterman 1931-1933

- Associated press All-Ohio Conference End, 1932

- Heidelberg College Varsity Football Captain 1933

- Associated Press Mythical Little All-American End (Honorable Mention), 1933

COMMENTS:

- Recipient of Oregon Distinguished Service Award, 1978 (the Distinguished Service Award is given to persons who by their knowledge and skills have made a significant contribution to the cultural development of Oregon or society as a whole.)

QUOTE:

- Heidelberg Aurora

"A toast to our captain "Chief" Bensell, a full-blooded American Indian, who gained the All-Ohio first team award at the close of his junior year. Every man who played with "Chief" will remember the constant smile, which soon became contagious. Toast a gentleman and a sport."

Peter Hauser

PETER "PETE" HAUSER
Inducted 1987

DATE OF BIRTH: 1884

DATE OF DEATH: July 21, 1935

BIRTH PLACE: El Reno, Oklahoma

TRIBE: Cheyenne

EDUCATION: Haskell Institute, Lawrence, Kansas

                Carlisle Indian School, Carlisle, Pennsylvania

SPORTS DATA: Football: Fullback

ACHIEVEMENTS:

- Varsity Football letterman, Haskell Indians, 1904 and 1905

- Varsity Football Letterman, Carlisle Indian School, 1906, 1907, 1908, 1909, 1910

- Captain, Carlisle Redskins Football Team, 1910

- All-American Honorable Mention, 1910

COMMENTS:

- Quote: Fabulous Redmen – Coach Warner was once asked by a Carlisle Herald reporter to name an All-Time Carlisle Indian Team. According to the reporter, Warner's choice for the position of fullback was Peter Hauser. Warner explained his selection by estimating the merits of each man.

- Hauser: Great fullback and passer. Hauser, who sometimes is credited with having thrown the first spiral pass, would hit his ends on the dead run with uncanny accuracy. Pete Hauser was practically a replica of Jim Thorpe. He was as good as Jim in all sports except track.

Mayes McLain

MAYES MC LAIN
Inducted 1987

DATE OF BIRTH: April 16, 1905

DATE OF DEATH: March 11, 1983

BIRTH PLACE: Pryor, Oklahoma

TRIBE: Cherokee

EDUCATION: Haskell Institute, Lawrence, Kansas

University of Iowa, Iowa City, Iowa

SPORTS DATA: Football

ACHIEVEMENTS:

- Haskell Indian Varsity Football Letterman, 1925-1926

- Member of team awarded a Special Gold Football with a cut diamond representing the 'Undefeated and Highest Scoring Team in the Nation' – The Haskell Indians of 1926

- McLain scored 253 points in the 1926 season. This was a single-season record, according to the Encyclopedia of Sport and the Guiness Book of Records.

- All-American Second – Team Fullback, 1926

- Collegiate High-Point Scorer of All-Time, 1926

- University of Iowa Varsity Football Letterman, 1927-1928

- Honor Selection to All-Western Second – Team Halfback, 1928

QUOTE:

- Haskell Annual 1927: "With a total of 558 points to their opponents' 63, the Indians were easily the high-point scorers of the world, while Mayes McLain, Indian fullback, set a new high-point record for all-time. As usual the Indians traveled from coast to coast during the course of the season. The All-Time, All-Haskell Indian Eleven named by Coach Richard "Dick" Hanley in 1926, showed Mayes McLain as his selection for fullback."

COMMENTS:

From 'Dayton Journal' 1926

- Before a game with Dayton: "the most feared man on the westerners' (Haskell) eleven is Mayes McLain, giant fullback, who is a terror with the ball, and one of the hardest hitting backs."

- After the game with Dayton: "If ever there was a one man football team Ted M. McLain is that individual."

Alex Sixkiller

ALEX "SONNY" SIXKILLER
Inducted 1987

DATE OF BIRTH: September 6, 1951

BIRTH PLACE: Tahlequah, Oklahoma

TRIBE: Cherokee

EDUCATION: University of Washington, Seattle, Washington

SPORTS DATA: Football

ACHIEVEMENTS:

- Washington "Husky" Varsity Football Letterman 1970-1972

- National Honor Selection to national NCAA Passing Champion as quarterback on Washington "Husky" Football Team 1970

- Co-Captain Washington "Husky" football Team 1971

- Co-Captain Washington "Husky" football Team 1972

- As Washington University Quarterback established Individual Career Records in the categories of Most Passes Attempted (811), Most Yards passing (5,496), Most Touchdown Passes

(35), Most Yards Total Offense (5,288). In 1970 completed 30 passes against University of Southern California in one game.

QUOTE:

- Los Angeles Times

"The Cherokee quarterback has captured the town (Seattle) without a struggle, because his arrows have hit often enough to bring the Washington Huskies back to foot ball respectability."

1989 INDUCTION

OKLAHOMA CITY, OKLAHOMA

Clarence Able

CLARENCE "TAFFY" ABEL

Inducted 1989

DATE OF BIRTH: May 21, 1901

DATE OF DEATH: August 1, 1964

BIRTH PLACE: Sault Ste. Marie, Michigan

TRIBE: Chippewa, Sault Ste. Marie Band

EDUCATION: Sault Area High School, Sault Ste. Marie, Michigan

SPORTS DATA: Hockey – Amateur and Professional

ACHIEVEMENTS:

Amateur Hockey Player – 1920-1926

- 1920-21 and 1921-22 hockey seasons, played with field's nationals, winning US Championship Title in the latter season.

- 1922-23 and 1923-24 hockey seasons, played with St. Paul Athletic Club as star defenseman.

- Selected as member of All-Star Hockey Team to represent the United States in 1924 Winter Olympic Games at Chamonix,

France. As captain and color bearer of the United States Team, he had the honor of carrying the Stars and Stripes in the Olympic parade and took the Olympic Oath for all the United States players.

- In 1925-26 hockey seasons, played with Minneapolis Millers and helped that team win the United States Championship title.

Professional Hockey Player – 1926-1934

- During 1926-27, 1927-28 and 1928-29 hockey seasons, played with the New York Rangers, in the latter season helping the Rangers win their first Stanley Cup.

- During the next five seasons, 1929 to 1934, played with Chicago Black Hawks. Established longest record of consecutive minutes played by any hockey player in playoff games in April, 1932, in which he played 110 minutes without relief. In the last game of 1934 playoffs, "Taffy" was the "Star Player", playing the full 60 minutes on the Chicago defense to bring the Black Hawks their first Stanley Cup. That year he established record for most minutes played in one season – 1,390 minutes with only 41 minutes on the penalty bench.

James Ingram

JAMES ARON INGRAM
Inducted 1989

DATE OF BIRTH: July 16, 1939

BIRTH PLACE: Enville, Oklahoma

TRIBE: Chickasaw

EDUCATION: Bacone College, Muskogee, Oklahoma

                   Oklahoma Christian College, Oklahoma City, Oklahoma

SPORTS DATA: Baseball, Track and Field, Basketball

ACHIEVEMENTS:

- Bacon College, 1958-1960:

    National Honor Award, First Team, All-American Baseball Squad of National Junior College Athletic Association.

    Baseball, All-Conference selection – First Team.

    Baseball, All-Star selection – Regional Tournament.

    Track and Field, First Place – 440 yard dash – Oklahoma Junior College Conference Meet. Tied Conference Record.

Track and Field, First Place – 440 yard dash – Regional Junior College Track Meet. Basketball, Varsity Letterman.

- Oklahoma Christian College 1961-1963:

1963 Established school records in half-mile, one-mile, two-mile, mile relay, sprint medley, and distance medley; received Outstanding Athlete Award in Track& Field.

1963 Honored with award of plaque at Oklahoma Christian College 10th Annual Relays as School Record Holder – 880 run, Mile Run, 2 mile run, Sprint Medley, and Distance Medley.

QUOTE:

- 1960 College Paper – "Personality of the Week is James Aron Ingram, a tall, dark, and handsome Chickasaw from Ardmore, Oklahoma. Active and outstanding in sports, he considers baseball to be his favorite. In addition to being President of the 'B' Club, he has twice been elected Student Senate Representative …. His ambitious and industrious mind revolves around chemistry teaching as a goal. Because of his congenial character and friendly disposition success is practically accomplished."

Euel Moore

EUEL WALTON "MONK" MOORE
Inducted 1989

DATE OF BIRTH: May 27, 1908

DATE OF DEATH: February 12, 1989

BIRTH PLACE: Reagan, Oklahoma

TRIBE: Chickasaw

EDUCATION: Grade School

SPORTS DATA: Baseball

ACHIEVEMENTS:

- Minor Leagues:

  Abeline, Texas – West Texas League 1929

  San Antonio, Texas – Texas League 1930-1932

  Galveston, Texas – Texas League 1933

  Baltimore Orioles – International League 1934

- Major Leagues:

  Philadelphia Phillies – National League 1934-1935

  New York Giants – National League 1935

  Philadelphia Phillies – National League 1936-1937

- Won his first major league victory July 8, 1934, Phillies vs Boston Braves, Score 5 to 3. Did not issue a base on balls and was tight in the pinches.

- Established reputation in the National League as a crafty and courageous hurler who could be sent up in the clinches as a pinch hitter. Hit .324 with the Orioles.

- Minor Leagues:

  Baltimore Orioles – International League 1938

  Dallas, Texas – Texas League 1939

  New Orleans, Louisiana – Southern Association 1940

QUOTE:

"In the Texas League, the big fellow hurled two No-Hit, No-Run contests and lost a heart-breaking One-Hitter with Baltimore when his opponent pitched a No-Hitter to beat him. In the latter game the first batter to face Moore pulled out a home run."

COMEMNTS:

- Won his first major league victory July 8, 1934, Phillies vs Boston Braves, Score 5 to 3. Did not issue a base on balls and was tight in the pinches.

- Established reputation in the National League as a crafty and courageous hurler who could be sent up in the clinches as a pinch hitter.

- Hit .324 with the Orioles.

- He began his pitching career in the minor leagues in 1927, and by 1933 had established himself as a world-class pitcher and Texas League workhorse, regularly pitching 300 innings a season, always with a sterling record. He began his major league career with the Philadelphia Phillies in 1934, but his career was cut short due to an injury sustained in spring training in 1935.

Alvin Williams

ALVIN LEROY WILLIAMS
Inducted 1989

DATE OF BIRTH: May 28, 1926

DATE OF DEATH: February 16, 1999

BIRTH PLACE: Verden, Oklahoma

TRIBE: Caddo

EDUCATION: Fort Cobb High School, Fort Cobb, Oklahoma

SPORTS DATA: Boxing – Amateur/Professional

ACHIEVEMENTS:

Amateur Boxer – 1944-1948

- Oklahoma State Golden Gloves and AAU Champion, Welterweight Division -1944

- Oklahoma State Golden Gloves and AAU Champion, Middleweight Division – 1947.

- Won Junior National AAU Middleweight Title and Advanced to semi-finals in Olympic Trials – 1947

- Oklahoma Golden Gloves and National Golden Gloves Champion, Middleweight Division. Won Oklahoma State and Regional Olympic Trials, Middleweight Division, and Advanced to quarter-finals in National Olympic Trials – 1948

Professional Boxer – 1949-1960

- As a professional middleweight and light-heavyweight boxer, fought 94 professional bouts, won 54 (24 by KO), 7 draws, and 33 losses, Ring Record Book – 1949-1960

- Won 13 straight fights and acclaimed "Prospect of the Month" in Ring Magazine – 1949

- Won Light-Heavyweight Title, State of Texas – 1953

- Fought Floyd Patterson, World Heavyweight Contender, in New York, NY, Moncton, Nebraska, Canada, and Kansas City, Kansas, losing by 8 round decision, 8 round TKO because of cut eye, and 3 round KO – 1954-1956

- Boxed exhibition matches with Floyd Patterson, Worlds heavyweight Titleholder, at Wichita, Kansas, and Little Rock, Arkansas – 1957

- Inducted in Oklahoma Athletic Hall of Fame in both championship rankings of Amateur and Professional Boxer – 1973

- Founded the American Indian new Life Boxing Club at Oklahoma City, Oklahoma, and received State (1980) and National (1981) honor selection as Golden Gloves Boxing Coach – 1975

1991 INDUCTION

LAWRENCE, KANSAS

John Allen

JOHN GENE "JOHNNY" ALLEN
Inducted 1991

DATE OF BIRTH: November 8, 1934

BIRTH PLACE: Pawnee, Oklahoma

TRIBE: Tonkawa/ Sac and Fox

EDUCATION: Oklahoma   A&M   College,   Stillwater, Oklahoma

Northeastern   State   College,   Tahlequah, Oklahoma

SPORTS DATA: Football, Basketball and Baseball

ACHIEVEMENTS:

- Oklahoma A&M College 1955-1956

  Varsity Letterman – Football

- Northeastern State College 1957-1958

  Varsity Letterman – Football, Basketball, and Baseball 1957

  Varsity Letterman – Football, Basketball, and Baseball 1958

Quarterback of "The Redmen", NAIA National Football Champions, won by "The Redmen" at St. Petersburg, Florida, in Holiday Bowl Game, December 20, 1958

Named by sports writers as "Most Valuable Player" and awarded NAIA Trophy as outstanding "Back of the Game" in the Holiday Bowl Game, December 20, 1958

- Played Professional Football with London Lords of Canadian League, London, Ontario, Canada 1959-1960

Named "Basketball Coach of the Year" Region 3, Oklahoma Coaches Association

QUOTE:

- St. Petersburg Times

"The Times award for MVP of the Holiday Bowl Game was a beautiful 21-jewel Lord Elgin watch. Allen was shocked on being selected for the lofty title. 'This is the biggest thrill I've ever had and, even though I need a watch, I think I'll just keep this one in the box to look at it.'"

Edwin Moore

EDWIN STANTON "ED" MOORE
Inducted 1991

DATE OF BIRTH: August 26, 1918

BIRTH PLACE: Morris, Oklahoma

TRIBE: Creek

EDUCATION: Chilocco Indian School, Newkirk, Oklahoma

                   Oklahoma A&M College, Stillwater, OK

SPORTS DATA: Football, Basketball

ACHIEVEMENTS:

- Chilocco Indian School 1933-1936

  Varsity Football Letterman – 1935

  Varsity Basketball Letterman – 1936

- Oklahoma A&M College 1937-1940

  Varsity Football Letterman 1938-1940

  Selected member All-Missouri Valley Conference Football Team 1939

All-Missouri Valley Conference Pass Receiving Leader 1939

All-American Honorable Mention 1939

QUOTE:

- Muskogee Daily Phoenix:

"Ed Moore, 185-pound end on the Oklahoma A&M College Football Team from Morris, was named end on the All-Missouri Valley Conference football team selected by the coaches of the conference this week. Moore, a junior in the school of education, is the best defensive wingman with the Aggies in years."

Andrew Payne

ANDREW HARTLEY "ANDY" PAYNE
Inducted 1991

DATE OF BIRTH: November 17, 1907

DATE OF DEATH: December 3, 1977

BIRTH PLACE: Foyil, Oklahoma

TRIBE: Cherokee

EDUCATION: Oklahoma City University

SPORTS DATA: Track/Cross Country

ACHIEVEMENTS:

- Track Star 1927

- At 3:46 pm, March 4, 1928, began "The great Cross-Country Marathon Race" from Los Angeles, California, to New York City, New York. Two hundred seventy-five runners began the race. Seventy runners made it to Chicago. Fifty-five struggled to reach the tape in Madison Square Garden, New York City, Saturday night May 26, 1928, ending the blistering race from ocean to ocean, sometimes called by the press "The Bunion Derby." The promoters said winning the marathon race would be "the most stupendous athletic accomplishment in all history." The race covered 3,422.3 miles, and "Andy" Payne was clocked at 573 hours, 4 minutes, and 34 seconds.

- First to cross the finish line, "Andy" Payne was awarded 1st prize of $25,000 and received national and international acclaim.

QUOTE:

- "The History of Rogers County, Oklahoma"

"In 1934, Andy was a successful candidate for Clerk of the Oklahoma Supreme Court. Always one to advocate self-improvement, Andy went to night school and earned his law degree from Oklahoma City University in 1953. The governor, legislators, other state officials, and thousands of friends honored this outstanding public servant on November 28, 1972, with a gigantic public reception at the State Capitol on what was officially proclaimed "Andy Payne Day.""

COMMENTS:

From "The Great American Foot Race – The Documentary"

- "Andy Payne, an Oklahoma Cherokee, was twenty years old when he decided to enter the 1928 Trans-Continental Foot Race. When asked why, Andy said "I just thought I could do it." Andy would finish in first place after the 84 day ordeal."

- THE GREAT AMERICAN FOOT RACE "documents an extraordinary 3,422-mile cross-country trek, won by 19 year old Cherokee Indian Andy Payne, the shy son of an Oklahoma farmer who entered the race because "I just thought I could do it." Dubbed "the Bunion Derby" by sports writers of the day, this was a grueling competition in which 199 runners attempted to cross the United States. Facing scorching temperatures, intermittent supplies of food and water, competing without modern running shoes or equipment, only 55 men finished the 84 day race from Los Angeles to

New York. The film not only describes Payne's incredible achievement, but tells the story of a race that was filled with drama, hucksterism, and even, unfortunately, the early beginnings of corporate sponsorship of athletic events."

1994 INDUCTION

ALBUQUERQUE
NEW MEXICO

Sammy Claphan

"SAMMY" JACK CLAPHAN
Inducted 1994

DATE OF BIRTH: October 10, 1956

DATE OF DEATH: November 26, 2001

BIRTH PLACE: Tahlequah, Oklahoma

TRIBE: Cherokee

EDUCATION: Stilwell High School, Stilwell, Oklahoma

University of Oklahoma, Norman, Oklahoma

SPORTS DATA: Football Amateur/Professional

ACHIEVEMENTS:

- 1970-74 Stilwell High School Football Team

- 1974 Named to three Oklahoma All-State Teams

- All-American High School Football Team by Parade Magazine

- Honorable Mention Big 8 Conference and Big Four Teams

- 1979 Played with Cleveland Browns

- 1981 Played with San Diego Chargers

Jackson Sundown

JACKSON SUNDOWN
Inducted 1994

DATE OF BIRTH: 1863

DATE OF DEATH: December 18, 1923

BIRTH PLACE: Idaho

TRIBE: Nez Perce

EDUCATION: Unknown

SPORTS DATA: Rodeo – Bronc Rider

ACHIEVEMENTS:

- Pendleton Round-Up, Pendleton, Oregon, captured the World championship in Bronc Riding at age 53, 1916

- First and only full-blood Indian ever to win a major rodeo championship

- Listed in Who's Who in Rodeo

- Inducted in Pendleton Round-Up Hall of Fame

COMMENTS: 'Lewiston Roundup Org.'

- "Jackson was entering rodeo events in Canada and Idaho. Tall, lean and handsome, he soon became a favorite of the crowds. He wore his hair in braids beneath his chin, and bright colored shirts.... By 1914, Waaya-Tonah-Toesits-Kahn was having so much success as an all-around rider, other cowboys were pulling out, refusing to ride against him. He began to give demonstrations using the name Buffalo Jackson. Sundown would often stay on horses and bulls until they came to a stop, and stock contractors began to remove their animals from competitions. Once ridden by Sundown, some animals would never buck again."

Mose Yellow Horse

MOSES J. YELLOWHORSE
Inducted 1994

DATE OF BIRTH: January 28, 1898

DATE OF DEATH: April 10, 1964

BIRTH PLACE: Pawnee, Oklahoma

TRIBE: Pawnee

EDUCATION: Pawnee Indian School, Pawnee, Oklahoma

                   Chilocco Indian School, Chilocco, Oklahoma

SPORTS DATA: Baseball – Amateur/Professional

ACHIEVEMENTS:

- Pitched for Ponca City Oilers at age 17 – 1917

- Pitched for Des Moines Team-League (folded due to WWI) – 1918

- Pitched for Little Rock Arkansas Travelers, helped the team to a pennant and a spot in the first Dixie Series – 1920

- Sold to Pittsburg Pirates – 1921

- Batting Average .315 – 1922

- Was among the best pitchers in Major Leagues listed in Who's Who in Professional Baseball

COMMENTS:

Elysian Fields Quarterly Review of Todd Fuller's 'The (Baseball) Life of Mose Yellowhorse'

- "Purchased by the Pirates in 1921, YellowHorse pitched well, at times exceptionally, over two seasons for a contending team whose roster included the eventual Hall of Famers Rabbit Maranville, Max Carey, and Pie Traynor. Possessed of scintillating heat, his fastball fetched comparison to Walter Johnson's; he was so effective coming out of the bullpen that Bucs fans continued to chant for him years after he'd left the team."

- "As Fuller notes, Rice's narrative is by far the 'most engaging and descriptive' of the three, spiced with such details as Cobb crowding the plate and sputtering racial slurs at Yellow Horse; the latter shaking off four signs from his catcher and then plunking Cobb between the eyes; and the Bucs rushing to protect their pitcher when the Tiger bench erupted."

- Elysian Fields Quarterly: "But as Fuller knows, a mere recounting of the highlights (and lowlights) of Yellow Horse's career is not what makes his saga so compelling. Of the many Native Americans who played in the majors, Mose was neither the first (Louis Sockalexis, Penobscot, starred in the 1890's with the Cleveland Spiders – later called Indians,) …nor the best (Charles "Chief" Bender, Ojibwa, pitched his way to Cooperstown; Allie "Superchief" Reynolds, Muscogee, tossed two no-hitters for the Yankees in 1951; Rudy York, Cherokee, was one of the American League's premier sluggers in the years just prior to World War II; and a half-dozen others had longer, more productive careers). And yet, when his day in the baseball sun was done, he returned to Pawnee and became a respected elder of his people, a keeper of tribal traditions and a source of pride to young and old. It's in the interviews with those who remember Mose, which Fuller conducted with genuine affection and respect, that we see and feel his real value – not just as a ballplayer but as a person, and not just as any person, but as a Native American beholden to his roots. "According to Stone Road, Yellow Horse counseled many young Pawnee men to carry out their lives in a responsible manner, to be true to their Pawnee heritage first, and to pursue personal achievements second," Fuller writes. "Even as Yellow Horse recognized the end of his life nearing, he reveled more in the celebration of tribal ceremonies than in his own baseball past."

1995 INDUCTION

LAWRENCE, KANSAS

Dawn Allen

DAWN KELLY ALLEN
Inducted 1995

DATE OF BIRTH: February 27, 1955

BIRTH PLACE: Lawton, Oklahoma

TRIBE: Quapaw/Cherokee/Euchee

EDUCATION: McClintock High School, Tempe, Arizona

Haskell Indian Junior College, Lawrence, Kansas

South Dakota State University

Arizona State University

SPORTS DATA: Tennis

ACHIEVEMENTS:

- Professional Tour 1990-1991

- National North American Indian Tennis Championships

    Women's Singles Champion: 1976-1984, 1986, 1988-1991

Women's Doubles Champion: 1977-1978, 1984-1986, 1990-1991

Mixed Doubles Champion: 1977-1978, 1984-1986, 1990-1991

- Worlds Fair All-Indian Tennis Tournament, Phoenix, Arizona

Women's Singles Champion: 1979

Women's Doubles Champion: 1979

- Arizona Indian Tennis Tournament, Phoenix, Arizona

Women's Singles Champion: 1979

Women's Doubles Champion: 1978-1979

Mixed Doubles Champion: 1978

- Creek Nation Indian Tennis Tournament, Okmulgee, Oklahoma

Women's Singles Champion: 1979

Women's Doubles Champion: 1979, 1980, 1988

Mixed Doubles Champion: 1988

QUOTE:

"Dawn is tireless when it comes to working with people of all ages. She has the capacity to recognize and respect each individual's strength and abilities, and to assist in developing outstanding Indian athletes of the future."

Her Mother: Patricia Daylight Allen

Karen Mackey

KAREN MACKEY
Inducted 1995

DATE OF BIRTH: July 30, 1956

BIRTH PLACE: Sioux City, Iowa

TRIBE: Santee Sioux

EDUCATION: East High School

Morning Side College, Sioux City, Iowa

SPORTS DATA: Judo

ACHIEVEMENTS:

- +78 kg US Open, 3rd , 1975

- Senior AAU Nationals Open, 3rd , 1976

- AAU International Open, 3rd , 1977

  +72 kg AAU International, 2nd

- National Championships Open, 3rd , 1978

- National Sports Festival III Open, 3rd

- US Open, 3rd , 1979

  National Championships Open, 2nd

- National Championships Open, 3rd , 1980

  Pan Am Trials Open, 3rd

- Olympic Sports Festival Open, 3rd , 1986

- +72 kg National Masters Competition, 1st , 1987

QUOTE:

- United States Judo Inc. President

  Ms Mackey has distinguished herself and gained recognition for the sport of Judo due to her accomplishments as a national and elite International Judo competitor, an outstanding representative for the sport and the United States.

Thomas Stidham

THOMAS EDWARD STIDHAM
Inducted 1995

DATE OF BIRTH: March 27, 1905

DATE OF DEATH: January 30, 1964

BIRTH PLACE: Checotah, Oklahoma

TRIBE: Creek

EDUCATION: Checota High School

                   Haskell Institute

                   University of Iowa

SPORTS DATA: Football, Coaching

ACHIEVEMENTS:

- Captain Haskell's undefeated football team, 1926

- East-West All Star football game, San Francisco played 60 minutes on offense and defense, 1927

- Assistant Coach at Northwestern University, 1928-32

- Line Coach at Northwestern University, 1933-34

- Head Coach at Oklahoma University, 1937-40

- Head Coach at Marquette University, 1941-45

- Line Coach at Green Bay Packers, 1946-49

- Newly completed student union building at Haskell built by students was named after Thomas Edward Stidham, Coach, 1965

QUOTE:

- Glenn "Pop" Warner, Stanford coach who saw the Haskell undefeated football team defeat the University of Hawaii 47 to 6 at San Francisco, pronounced Stidham and Roebuck as fine a pair of tackles as he had ever seen.

1996 INDUCTION

PHOENIX, ARIZONA

Ryneldi Becenti

RYNELDI BECENTI
Inducted 1996

DATE OF BIRTH: August 11, 1971

BIRTH PLACE: Fort Defiance, Arizona

TRIBE: Navajo

EDUCATION: Window Rock High School, Window Rock, Arizona

Scottsdale Community College, Scottsdale, Arizona

Arizona State University, Tempe, Arizona

SPORTS DATA: Basketball

ACHIEVEMENTS:

- 1986-89 Arizona High School All-State

- 1987-88 Arizona High School Player of the Year

- 1988-89 High School All-American

- 1990-91 Junior College All-American

- 1991-93 All Conference Pac 10 Team

- 1992-93 All-American Honorable Mention Arizona State University

- 1993 Bronze Medal winner as member of USA team in World University Games

- 1994 Professional Basketball – Sweden

COMMENTS:

- Arizona State University Athletic Hall of Fame:

"Women's Basketball / 1992-1993 Ryneldi Becenti was a two-time honorable mention All-American honoree while also becoming one of only three Sun Devils to earn All-Pac-10 first team honors twice in a career. Following two successful seasons at Scottsdale Community College, she took to the hardwood with the Sun Devils and in two seasons, recording the second-most assists in an ASU career with 396. The school record holder with 17 assists in one game, her 7.1 helpers per contest stands, as the best average all-time in the Pac-10 Conference. With 15 points, 10 rebounds and 12 assists in a Jan. 25, 1992 game with Oregon State, Becenti became the first player in school history to record a triple-double and also was the lone player in the NCAA, including the men, to record the feat that season. A member of the American Indian Athletic Hall of Fame, she earned her bachelor's degree in sociology in 1997."

Dr. George Blue Spruce

DR. GEORGE BLUE SPRUCE JR.
Inducted 1996

DATE OF BIRTH: January 16, 1931

BIRTH PLACE: Santa Fe, New Mexico

TRIBE: San Juan Laguna Pueblo

EDUCATION: St. Michael's High School, Santa Fe, New Mexico

Creighton University, Omaha, Nebraska

SPORTS DATA: Tennis

ACHIEVEMENTS:

- Santa Fe, New Mexico High School City Championships – 1949

- Captain Creighton University Tennis Team – 1950-1953

- Won Tennis Championships during his tour of duty as a dentist in the US Navy – 1956-1958

- Assistant tennis coach at US Merchant Marine Academy and competed in sanctioned tournaments – 1963-1966

- Won Men's Open Singles in the North American Indian Tennis Championships – 1977

- Gold Medals in both Phoenix and Arizona State Senior Olympics in tennis in the 50- 55 age category – 1983-1984

- Dr. Blue Spruce has won singles titles in the 35 and 45 age categories and holds double titles teaming with other American Indian individuals – 1980's

- Dr. Blue Spruce has been past president of the North American Indian Tennis Association and has served on the Board of Directors.

John Sellers

JOHN R. SELLERS
Inducted 1996

DATE OF BIRTH: January 29, 1945

BIRTH PLACE: Tahlequah, Oklahoma

TRIBE: Cherokee

EDUCATION: Tahlequah High School, Tahlequah, Oklahoma

Northeastern State College (University), Tahlequah, Oklahoma

SPORTS DATA: Baseball, Basketball

ACHIEVEMENTS:

- Four year Letterman in Baseball and Basketball 1962

- Baseball All-Conference 1964-1966

- Baseball NAIA All-American 1965-1966

- Led team in home runs, triples, doubles, singles and tied for most stolen bases 1962-1966

- Oklahoma National Indian Athletic Association State Champions 1974-1978

- All-Star Team NIAA Championships 1974-1978

- International softball congress Fast Pitch State Champions and MVP 1976

- ISC State Champions and MVP 1978

- American Softball Association State Champions and MVP 1980

- All-Star Shortstop, Saskatchewan, CN1982

- MVP 37 times in US and Canada tournaments.

1997 INDUCTION

OKLAHOMA CITY, OKLAHOMA

Mike Edwards

MIKE EDWARDS
Inducted 1997

DATE OF BIRTH: 1961

BIRTH PLACE: Tulsa, Oklahoma

TRIBE: Cherokee/Choctaw/Chickasaw

EDUCATION: Edison High School, Tulsa, Oklahoma

                   Tulsa Jr. College, Tulsa, Oklahoma

                   OKC Community College, Oklahoma City,
                   Oklahoma

SPORTS DATA: Bowling

ACHIEVEMENTS:

- 1979 Won Boys Open Division Scholarship Championship, Chickasaw, Oklahoma

- 1984 Six – 2nd Place Finishes in PBA career

- 1985 Won Bowlers Journal World Doubles Championship, Tulsa, Oklahoma

- 1989 Named to Bowlers Journal Magazine's 3rd Team All-American Squad; 2nd Place in ABC Bud Light Master's Tournament, Wichita, KS; 6th Place in BPAA U.S. Open Championship Edmond, OK

- 1991 One of four Pros in PBA history to participate in four Consecutive ABC sport championship round Telecasts; 4th Place Showboat Invitational, Las Vegas, NV; 3rd Pace ARC Open, Pinole, CA; 2nd Place, Quaker State Open, Grand Prairie, TX; 2nd Place, Florida Open, Winter Haven, FL

- 1992 Established 3 game series record for State of Oklahoma with a 869 series; 290- 279-300, Edmond, OK

- 1993 Co-holder of PBA Record for highest single match game score – a 300 – 300 Tie against David Ozio, San Antonio, TX; Featured in ABC Bowling magazine entitled "The Year of the Indian"

- 1994 Won first Pro Bowlers Assoc. Title at IOF Foresters Bowling for Miracles Open, Toronto, Ontario

- 1995 Ranked in top 40 on PBA All-time money list. He has bowled 26 perfect games – 12 during PBA tour and 14 sanctioned league and tournament events.

James Johnson

JAMES LAWRENCE JOHNSON
"Waukechon"
Inducted 1997

DATE OF BIRTH: March 28, 1909

DATE OF DEATH: September 3, 1972

BIRTH PLACE: Odanah, Wisconsin

TRIBE: Menominee

EDUCATION: Haskell Institute, Lawrence, Kansas

SPORTS DATA: Football

ACHIEVEMENTS:

- Haskell Institute – 1929

- Boston Redskins – 1933-1935

- New York Yankees – 1936

- New York Giants, World Champions in 1938 – 1936-1939

- Washington Redskins – 1944

Jimmie Keel

JIMMIE EARL KEEL
Inducted 1997

DATE OF BIRTH: December 12, 1929

BIRTH PLACE: Stratford, Oklahoma

TRIBE: Chickasaw

EDUCATION: Chilocco Indian Agricultural School 1946

                             Cameron College, Lawton, Oklahoma 1949

                             Central State University, Edmond, Oklahoma 1957

SPORTS DATA: Boxing – Amateur/Professional

ACHIEVEMENTS:

- Three year letterman, Boxing, Chilocco Indian School 1944-1946

- Oklahoma Northeastern Golden Glove Champion, 1946

- Oklahoma State AAU Champion, 1947-1949

- National AAU Finalist, 1947-1948

- Oklahoma State Golden Glove Champion, 1948

- Cameron Jr. College Boxing Team – Letterman 1948-1949

- Coach, Cameron JC Boxing Team 1949

- Professional Boxing Career; won 67 fights and lost 14, 1950

COMMENTS:

- Spent 36 years in the Squared Circle; Served as Fighter, Judge, Trainer and Referee.

- As a Referee, Keel was the Third Man in the Ring with such notables as Sonny Liston, Cleveland Williams, George Foreman, and Cassus Clay.

2000 INDUCTION

TULSA, OKLAHOMA

Perry Beaver

R. PERRY BEAVER
Inducted 2000

DATE OF BIRTH: December 13, 1938

BIRTH PLACE: Muskogee, Oklahoma

TRIBE: Muscogee/Creek

EDUCATION: Morris High School, Morris, Oklahoma

                   Murray State Junior College, Tishmingo,
                   Oklahoma

                   Northeast Louisiana University, Monroe,
                   Louisiana

                   University of Central Oklahoma, Edmond,
                   Oklahoma

                   Northeastern State University, Tahlequah,
                   Oklahoma

SPORTS DATA: Football, Coaching

ACHIEVEMENTS:

- 1955 Morris High School, All-Conference, All-District, Honorable Mention All-State

- 1958 Murray State Jr. College, All-American

- 1959-1960 Northeastern LA University, All-Conference, Outstanding Center-Linebacker

- 1961 Professional, Green Bay Packers – Coached by Legendary Vince Lombardi

- 1975 Tulsa World Coach of the Year – Successful Football coach Jenks Oklahoma with a 109-53 Record, 8 district titles, 7 Area Championships and 2 State Titles in 25 years

- 1991 Inducted into the Oklahoma Coaches Hall of Fame

- 1998 Inducted into the Northeast LA Hall of Fame

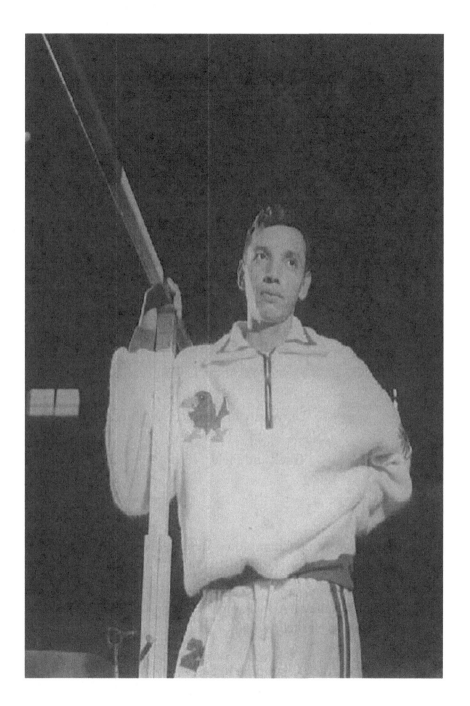

Robert Cannon

ROBERT J. CANNON
Inducted 2000

DATE OF BIRTH: February 7, 1931

DATE OF DEATH: February 11, 2003

BIRTH PLACE: Arkansas City, Kansas

TRIBE: Osage

EDUCATION: Haskell Institute, Lawrence, Kansas

University of Kansas, Lawrence, Kansas

SPORTS DATA: Track and Field

ACHIEVEMENTS:

- State High Jump Champion – Repeatedly set new records at Various Meets for Haskell – 1949

- Missouri Valley AAU Champion – Won 1st Place in 18 out of 19 Meets at Haskell – 1950

- All-Japan track Champion in Sasbo, Japan – 1953

- Won Kansas Relays High Jump, University of Kansas, Continued to Set New Records – 1956

- Big 8 Outdoor Champion, University of Kansas – 1958

- Big 8 Indoor Champion, University of Kansas, Won 1st Place in all 8 Meets – 1959

- Kansas Relays Champion, University of Kansas, Member of KU Coach Bill Easton's Grand Slam Track & Field Teams that were undefeated in Conference History – 1959

- Big 8 Outdoor Champion, University of Kansas – 1959

Andrew Sockalexis

ANDREW SOCKALEXIS
Inducted 2000

DATE OF BIRTH: January 11, 1892

DATE OF DEATH: August 26, 1919

BIRTH PLACE: Indian Island, Maine

TRIBE: Penobscot

EDUCATION: Old Town High School, Old Town, Maine

SPORTS DATA: Marathon Runner

ACHIEVEMENTS:

- 1911   1st Place Bangor Maine 5 Mile Run

- 1912   2nd Place Bangor Maine 20 Mile Run

- 1912-1913 2nd Place Boston Marathon – first Maine Athlete to compete in modern Olympics, 4th Place finish Stockholm Olympics – American Marathon Team

- 1913   Became professional runner

- 1984   Inducted into the Maine Sports Hall of Fame

- 1991   Inducted into the Maine Running Hall of Fame

COMMENTS:

- Boston Athletic Association 1912 Boston Marathon "U.S. Olympic bound marathoner Mike Ryan of New York ran through a mud and slush filled course to finish first in 2:21:18 and take 21 seconds off DeMar's one year old record. Ryan was content to let Yale freshman Johnny Gallagher set the early pace. As Gallagher tired near Cleveland Circle, Andrew Sockalexis, a young Indian runner from Old Town, Maine, took over the lead. Ryan caught Sockalexis two miles from the finish and won by 34 seconds."

- Boston Athletic Association 1913 Boston Marathon "For the second consecutive year the "Maine Indian" Andrew Sockalexis was the runner-up. Knowing he had raced too hard in the early going the previous year, Sockalexis let Swedish born Fritz Carlson set the early pace. Carlson was four minutes ahead of Sockalexis with four miles remaining when the runners hit Cleveland Circle. Carlson held off a valiant rush by Sockalexis over the final few miles to win the race in 2:25:14."

Louis Sockalexis

LOUIS SOCKALEXIS
Inducted 2000

DATE OF BIRTH: October 24, 1871

DATE OF DEATH: December 24, 1913

BIRTH PLACE: Indian Island, Maine

TRIBE: Penobscot

EDUCATION: Old Town High School, Old Town, Maine

St. Mary's College, Van Buren, Maine

Holy Cross College, Worcester, Maine

Notre Dame University, South Bend, Indiana

SPORTS DATA: Baseball

ACHIEVEMENTS:

- First Native American to Play Professional Baseball

- 1894-1895 Batted .444 over two seasons – spectacular home runs, stole 6 bases in one game

- 1897 Batted .338 for Cleveland Spiders (Indians) – Cleveland changed their name in honor of Louis F. Sockalexis – touted the Most Popular Player in the league

- 1956 Inducted into the Holy Cross Athletic Hall of Fame

- 1969 Charter Member of the Maine Baseball Hall of Fame

- 1985 Inducted into the Maine Sports Hall of Fame

2004 INDUCTION

TULSA, OKLAHOMA

Howard Hatch

HOWARD GAYLE HATCH
Inducted 2004

DATE OF BIRTH: May 7, 1939

BIRTH PLACE: Muskogee, Oklahoma

TRIBE: Delaware

EDUCATION: Baton Rouge Catholic High School

Northwestern State, Louisiana

SPORTS DATA: Weightlifting Coach, Basketball

ACHIEVEMENTS:

- 1961 Started in Basketball at Northwestern State (LA)

- Twelve-time National Coach of the Year (weightlifting),

- Hatch is a U.S.A. Senior, U.S. International Coach who served as "Credentials Coach" (90KG class) at the 1988 and 1992 Olympic Games

- Served as head coach for the 1989 Junior World Team and head coach for the 1989 Pan Am Team

- "Meet Director" for the 2000 Olympic weightlifting trials at Alario Center, Westwego

- USA Olympic Weightlifting Hall of Fame (April, 2001)

- USA Strength Coaches Hall of Fame (April, 2003)

- Northwestern State University Athletic Hall of Fame (February, 2003)

- USA Masters Weightlifting Hall of Fame (April, 2002)

- Louisiana Weightlifting Hall of Fame (June, 2003)

- Louisiana Strength & Conditioning Hall of Fame (May, 2003)

COMMENTS:

- Coach Hatch's weightlifting team members have been selected to forty-one (two of these were in the Olympics) U.S. International teams and won forty-three national Championships. He coached Tommy Calandro (1984 Olympian) as well as Bret Brian (1988 and 1992 Olympian).

- In December 1961, he scored forty-four points against Kentucky Wesleyan; they were ranked third in the nation. Hatch's 18 field goals made out of twenty-one attempts in that game are not only still a school record but also ranks as one of college basketball's all-time best.

Dr. Larry Ramirez

LARRY JOE RAMIREZ
Inducted 2004

DATE OF BIRTH: July 24, 1947

BIRTH PLACE: Riverside, California

TRIBE: Pascua Yaqui/Chiricahua Apache

EDUCATION: Gary High School, Pomona, California

Mt. San Antonio Jr. College

California State Northridge

International University, San Diego, CA

SPORTS DATA: Baseball – Amateur

ACHIEVEMENTS:

- Selected to American Legion All-Star Team 1962-1963

- All League (California Collegiate Athletic Association); selected by Coaches to Topps All-District and Honorable Mention All-American and CCAA Player of the year; Played in Summer College All-Star League in South Dakota; Selected as one of top players in the country; Pitched 4 consecutive games and helped win Basin league Title for Rapid City Chiefs. 1969

- Pitched a 5 hitter, striking out 10 in College World Series to help win the National Championship; still holds record for best ERA with 2.00. In top 5 with best ERA for a Season with 1.84 and tops in complete games and shutouts. 1969

Jim Warne

JIM E. WARNE, JR.
Inducted 2004

DATE OF BIRTH: November 27, 1964

BIRTH PLACE: Phoenix, Arizona

TRIBE: Oglala Lakota Sioux

EDUCATION: Tempe Union High School, Tempe, Arizona

                   Arizona State University

                   San Diego State

SPORTS DATA: Football – Amateur/Professional

ACHIEVEMENTS:

- Helped lead Sun Devils to first Rose bowl with a 22-15 victory over Michigan 1987

- Voted All-Pac 10 Second Team (Portland, Oregon)

- Voted All-Pac 10 Honorable mention (Coaches Poll)

- Played in 41st Annual Hula Bowl, Hawaii

- Drafted by Bengals – Played in 3 Strike Games

- Signed as Free Agent with Buccaneers for 2 ½ years 1988

- Signed with NY/NJ Knights North American East Division Champions as an Offensive Lineman 1991

2006 INDUCTION

SANTA FE, NEW MEXICO

Stephen Gachupin

STEPHEN GACHUPIN
Inducted 2006

DATE OF BIRTH: September 1, 1942

BIRTH PLACE: Jemez Pueblo, New Mexico

TRIBE: Walatowa Pueblo of Jemez

EDUCATION: Jemez Valley High School

                   New Mexico State University

SPORTS DATA: Marathon, Distance Runner

ACHIEVEMENTS:

- 1969 World Masters Marathon (Las Vegas, Nevada – 1969) second among American runners and 5th over-all.

- 1969 Won Western Hemisphere Marathon, Culver City California

- Six time winner of the Pikes Peak Run – a record for most wins. Consecutive wins from 1966-1971.

- Five time winner of the LaLuz Trail Run (Sandia Mountain) 1966.1967, 1968, 1970, 1979

- Numerous marathons

- Coaching

Emmitt Peters

EMMITT G. PETERS, SR.
Inducted 2006

DATE OF BIRTH: October 1, 1940

BIRTH PLACE: Ruby, Alaska

TRIBE: Athabascan

EDUCATION: Mt. Edgecumbe High School, Sitka, Alaska

                   Northrup Institutes

SPORTS DATA: Dog Musher

ACHIEVEMENTS:

- Won the Iditarod 1000+ mile race setting a new record,

  14 days/14 hours/43 min./15 sec. 1975

  Last rookie to win the Iditarod over the past 30 years.

- Finished 5th in the Iditarod, 1975

- Finished 4th in the Iditarod, 1976

- Finished 3rd in the Iditarod, 1977

- Finished 2nd in the Iditarod, 1978

- Finished 9th in the Iditarod, 1979

- Finished 12th in the Iditarod, 1980

- Finished 4th in the Iditarod, 1981

- Finished 19th in the Iditarod, 1982

- Finished 17th in the Iditarod, 1983

- Finished 12th in the Iditarod, 1984

- Finished 41st in the Iditarod, 1990

COMMENTS:

- Official Site of the Iditarod

"Its unlike any other event in the world. A race over 1,150 miles of the most extreme and beautiful terrain known to man: across mountain ranges, frozen rivers, dense forests, desolate tundra and windswept coastline …. The race pits man and animal against nature, against wild Alaska at her best …. There are names which are automatically associated with the race …. Herbie Nayokpuk, Shishmaref; Emmitt Peters, Ruby; whose record set in 1975 was not broken until 1980, when Joe May, Trapper Creek, knocked seven hours off the record …."

Aloysuis Waquie

ALOYSUIS "AL" WAQUIE
Inducted 2006

DATE OF BIRTH: June 15, 1954

BIRTH PLACE: Jemez Pueblo, New Mexico

TRIBE: Walatowa Pueblo of Jemez

EDUCATION: Jemez Valley High School

Haskell Indian Jr. College

SPORTS DATA: Cross Country, Distance Runner

ACHIEVEMENTS:

- 1971   Cross Country All American at Haskell Indian Jr. College

- La Luz Trail Run (Sandia Peak) 8 time winner and Record Holder.

- Empire State Building Run 5 time winner and Record Holder.

- Two time winner and set new record of the Pikes Peak Run.

- AAU Athlete of the Month August 1978.

- Sports Illustrated Merit Award 1980.

- Popay Tricentennial Award 1980.

2007 INDUCTION

TULSA, OKLAHOMA

Dr. Noah Allen

DR. NOAH G. ALLEN
Inducted 2007

DATE OF BIRTH: November 14, 1927

BIRTH PLACE: Bristow, Oklahoma

TRIBE: Creek / Euchee

EDUCATION: Quapaw High School, Quapaw, Oklahoma
                    1947

                    Wichita University – BA Degree 1950

                    Kansas State University, Pittsburg – MS
                    Degree 1957

                    University of Oregon – Doctor of Education
                    Degree 1965

SPORTS DATA: Coaching, Athletic Administration

ACHIEVEMENTS:

- 1960 Assistant Coach – New Mexico State University. Won Sun Bowl in El Paso, Texas.

- 1961 Athletic Director, Head Football and Tennis Coach at Pacific University, Forest Grove, Oregon. Tennis Team was ranked in the top 10 teams in the Nation three years in succession by the National Inter-Collegiate Athletic Association.

- Served as the President of the National Inter-Collegiate Tennis Coaches Association. President of the Northwest Conference football Coaches Association.

- 1965 to 1968 Athletic Director , Wichita State University. Chairman of the Missouri Valley Athletic Director's Association. Athletic Program ranked the best in the Missouri Valley Conference two years in succession. Basketball team reached the final four, also played in the National Invitation Tournament and was selected by the US State Department to tour South America on a goodwill exhibition tour.

- 1971 Head football, tennis coach and Athletic Director, Haskell Indian Junior College, Lawrence, Kansas.

William Breddé

WILLIAM "BILL" M. BREDDÉ
Inducted 2007

DATE OF BIRTH: December 31, 1932

DATE OF DEATH: September 19, 2006

BIRTH PLACE: Quechan Indian Reservation near Yuma, Arizona

TRIBE: Quechan / Pawnee

EDUCATION: Pawnee High School, Oklahoma

                   Oklahoma A & M (Oklahoma State University) - Education

SPORTS DATA: Football

ACHIEVEMENTS:

- 1954 Played offense and defense for four years for the Oklahoma A & M Cowboys. He was a super star on defense and special teams. Led the Cowboys to a 7 – 2 season in 1954. He returned the kickoff 98 yards against the Oklahoma Sooners.

- Led his team in Punt – returns, and interceptions 3 successive years. Led his team in kickoff returns two years.

- 1954 Selected to play in College All-Star Game at Soldier Field in Chicago, Illinois. Played in the Shrine East – West Game at Kezar Stadium in San Francisco, California. Played in the Blue – Gray College All-Star Game in Montgomery, Alabama.

- In 1954 "Pawnee" Bill Breddé was the fourth round draft pick of the Chicago Cardinals of the National Football League. He was the 37th player picked in the draft. He played in 12 games for the Cardinals. He played on offense and defense.

- Special Honors – Named to Oklahoma State University's All Century Foot ball Team.

Edward Burgess

EDWARD "EDDIE" BURGESS
Inducted 2007

DATE OF BIRTH: June 17, 1890

DATE OF DEATH: July 25, 1923

BIRTH PLACE: Schulter, Oklahoma

TRIBE: Creek / Cherokee

EDUCATION: Unknown

SPORTS DATA: Rodeo – Calf & Steer Roper

ACHIEVEMENTS:

- 1919 Calgary Stampede Rodeo, Calgary, Canada

- Eddie was among the top money winners in many major rodeos including: Calgary and Winnipeg, Canada, Cheyenne and Laramie, Wyoming; Chicago, Illinois; New York City, New York; and Denver, Colorado in the United States.

- Tragedy struck the "Wizard of the Lariat" before 10,000 fans! Eddie Burgess lost his life while roping a steer at the Cheyenne Frontier Days Rodeo. "Rex" his favorite roping horse accidentally fell on him after losing his footing while stopping a big steer!

Michael Gregory

MICHAEL DEAN GREGORY
Inducted 2007

DATE OF BIRTH: May 16, 1947

BIRTH PLACE: Oklahoma City, Oklahoma

TRIBE: Creek / Euchee

EDUCATION: Midwest City High School, University of Oklahoma – BA Degree Journalism

SPORTS DATA: Track – Long Jump, Sprint Relays and Low Hurdles

ACHIEVEMENTS:

- 1966

Kansas State Indoor Relays – 1st Long Jump

Big 8 Freshman Postal Meet – Indoor & Outdoor 1st Place Long Jump

Kansas Relays – 1st Place in 440 & 880 yard Relay – tied National Record in 440 Relay

- 1967

  Kansas Relays – 1st Long Jump

  Dallas Invitational Indoor meet – 1st Long Jump

  Big 8 Outdoor Meet – 4th Long Jump

- 1968

  All American in the Long Jump

  NCAA indoor meet – 2nd Long Jump

  Drake Relays – 2nd Long Jump

  John Jacobs Invitational meet – 1st Long Jump

- 1969

  Northeast Louisiana Indoor meet – 1st Long Jump

  Big 8 Indoor Meet – 2nd Long Jump

  NCAA Indoor Meet – 5th Long Jump

- A Distinguished Military Graduate of the University of Oklahoma ROTC Program

Pete Shephard

PETE W. SHEPHERD
Inducted 2007

DATE OF BIRTH: July 24, 1908

DATE OF DEATH: December 28, 1990

BIRTH PLACE: Flandreau, South Dakota

TRIBE: Santee Sioux

EDUCATION: Flandreau High School, Flandreau, SD

Haskell Institute, Lawrence, KS

Chillicothe Business College, Chillicothe, MO – BA Degree

University of Oklahoma, Norman, OK – MA Degree

SPORTS DATA: Football

ACHIEVEMENTS:

- Football Quarterback and Defensive Linebacker, on Haskell Institutes greatest teams! Intercepted four passes in one game.

Was identified as the best blocker in the country while playing for the Haskell Indians! 1928-1931

COMMENTS:

- Ability, Integrity, Sportsmanship and Character, Pete Shepherd had them all!

- A Great leader in Indian Education.

2008 INDUCTION

NIAGARA FALLS, NEW YORK

William Arams

WILLIAM "GUMPS" ABRAMS
Inducted 2008

DATE OF BIRTH: March 5, 1925

DATE OF DEATH: January 14, 2005

BIRTH PLACE: Quaker Bridge, New York

TRIBE: Seneca

EDUCATION: Gowanda High School, Jamestown Community College – AA Degree Political Science

SPORTS DATA: Lacrosse

ACHIEVEMENTS:

ATHLETIC ACHIEVEMENTS:

- Lacrosse League Champions, Rochester, New York 1948-1949

- Lacrosse League Champions, Detroit, Michigan 1952

- League leading scorer 1952

- Inducted into the Lacrosse Hall of Fame Ontario Canada, 1958

- Seneca Nation Lacrosse Hall of Fame named in his honor

OTHER ACHIEVEMENTS:

- Served in the United States Navy during World War II and was honored for his Naval Service by Senator Daniel Inouye when he presented a commendation to him in Washington DC

- Mr. Abrams worked for his Tribe in numerous assignments such as: Seneca Nation Tribal Councilor, Seneca Nation Head Game Warden, Seneca Representative to the New York State Office on aging, became an Eagle Scout and served as a Scout Master for many years.

- Mr. Abrams lived a remarkable life in service to his Tribe

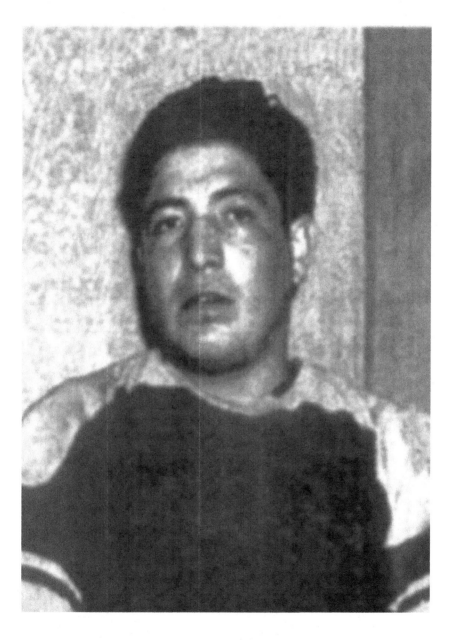

Nelson Huff

NELSON "BALLY" HUFF
Inducted 2008

DATE OF BIRTH: August 24, 1924

BIRTH PLACE: Newtown Community – Cattaraugus
                   Territory, Lawtons, NY

TRIBE: Seneca

EDUCATION: Gowanda High School

SPORTS DATA: Lacrosse

ACHIEVEMENTS:

- North American Lacrosse Association High Scorer: 1950, 1951, 1952 and 1953

- North American Lacrosse Association Most Valuable Player: 1950 and 1951

- Newtown Golden Eagles Lacrosse Coach: 1966, 1967 and 1968

- Coach of North American Lacrosse All-Stars, Canadian Expo-Montreal Canada: 1968

- Inducted into the Ontario Lacrosse Hall of Fame in 2005

OTHER ACHIEVEMENTS:

- Was a great scorer with either his left or right hand and had blazing speed

- It is said by his peers that he is the most skilled "all around" athlete to have played the sport of Lacrosse. He had the speed, quickness, coordination and the ability to weave through the defense to score. His skill and determination set an example for teammates.

- Nelson "Bally" Huff could do it all in the sport of Lacrosse. He has been a credit to his team, to his family and community and to the Seneca Nation of Indians

Oren Lyons

OREN LYONS
Inducted 2008

DATE OF BIRTH: March 5, 1930

BIRTH PLACE: Cattaraugus Territory

TRIBE: Onondaga

EDUCATION: Syracuse University – Bachelor of Fine Arts 1958

SPORTS DATA: Lacrosse

ACHIEVEMENTS:

- Four year Letterman in Lacrosse at Syracuse University

- All American in Lacrosse 1957 and 1958

- Syracuse University Hall of Fame 1988

- National Lacrosse Hall of Fame 1993

- Ontario Canada Lacrosse Hall of Fame 1998

- Upstate New York Chapter of USA Lacrosse Hall of Fame 2000

OTHER ACHIEVEMENTS:

- "Orange Key Award" Outstanding Student 1957, Syracuse University

- Syracuse University "Letter Winner of Distinction", 1990

- Stockholm University School of Business "Sustainable Leader of the Year" 1998

- United Nation's "International World Peace Prize"

- Syracuse University building named in his honor "Lyons Residence Hall"

- Faith Keeper – Onondaga Longhouse – Turtle Clan

David Powless

DAVID A. POWLESS
Inducted 2008

DATE OF BIRTH: May 29, 1943

BIRTH PLACE: Ottawa, Illinois

TRIBE: Oneida

EDUCATION: Rock Island High School, Illinois

                   University of Oklahoma, 1961

                   University of Illinois, 1966, Bachelor's Degree
                   Marketing and Economics

SPORTS DATA: Football

ACHIEVEMENTS:

- National Champions, 1962

- Played in the 1963 Rose Bowl

- Drafted by the New York Giants (National Football League)
  and by the Kansas City Chief's (American Football League)

- Played Professional Football for the New York Giants and the
  Washington Redskins

OTHER ACHIEVEMENTS:

- Very successful business man: Owned and operated Insurance business with Hall of Fame Football Player Dick Butkus

- Recognized as "The Small Business Administration National Innovation Advocate of the Year Award at the White House in Washington, DC

2009 INDUCTION

MAYETTA, KANSAS

Warner Coffin, Jr.

WARNER A. "TONY" COFFIN JR.
Inducted 2009

DATE OF BIRTH: October 10, 1916

DATE OF DEATH: September 25, 1966

BIRTH PLACE: Mayetta, Kansas

TRIBE: Potawatomi

EDUCATION: Mayetta High School

University of Kansas, Bachelor Degree

SPORTS DATA: Athletic Administration, Coaching

ACHIEVEMENTS:

- Baseball Letterman, University of Kansas

- Coached Billy Mills – 1964 Olympic 10,000 meter Champion

- Coached Dr. John Edwards – who set a new record in the indoor 60 yard dash

- Received the Department of the Interiors highest honor – "The Distinguished Service Award" in Washington, DC

- The new athletic facility at Haskell Indian Nations University was named in his honor

- Partial Coaching records

    o Basketball – 106 wins, 30 losses

    o Football – 25 wins, 5 losses

    o Track and Field – Two state Championships, Second in state one time, Third is state one time

- Coach Coffin's records on the field were indeed impressive, but his record off the field was astounding! He taught honesty, pride, perseverance, respect, loyalty, controlled aggressiveness, sportsmanship, and pride in their Indian Heritage, initiative and punctuality. Tony Coffin lived his short life as an example for his family and the student athletes he touched.

Joseph Hipp

JOSEPH T. "JOE" HIPP
Inducted 2009

DATE OF BIRTH: December 7, 1962

BIRTH PLACE: Browning, Montana

TRIBE: Blackfeet

EDUCATION: Davis High School 1981

SPORTS DATA: Boxer

ACHIEVEMENTS:

- Won World Boxing Federation (WBF) Heavyweight Championship of the World.

- Won World Boxing Federation (WBF) Intercontinental Heavyweight Championship

- Won North American Boxing Federation (NABF) Heavyweight Championship

- Ranked #2 in the world by the IBF, number 3 in the world by the WBC, 1995

- Fought for the WBA World Heavyweight Championship in August 1995 (Fight stopped, round 10, due to cut).

- First Native American heavyweight boxer to be rated in the top 10 in the world

- First Native American to win the North American Heavyweight Title (NABF)

- First Native American to win a World Heavyweight Title

- Defended NABF Title and relinquished title undefeated

- First Native American to fight for a World Heavyweight Championship (August 19, 1995 and June 25, 1999)

- Won Western States Championship (Sanctioned by the American Professional Boxing Association)

Melvin Peterson

MELVIN ARTHUR PETERSON "PETE"

Inducted 2009

DATE OF BIRTH: October 20, 1966

BIRTH PLACE: San Juan, Puerto Rico

TRIBE: Cherokee

EDUCATION: Aquinas High School, 1985

North Greenville Junior College

Georgia State University, Bachelor in Business Administration 1990

SPORTS DATA: Tennis

ACHIEVEMENTS:

- First Team All-Region 10 National Junior College Athletic Association, 1986

- Member of NCJAA Co-Championship Team, 1987

- Most Valuable Player Award NGJC, 1987

- Member, Championship Team – Trans-America Athletic Conference, 1989

- Awarded All-Conference recognition, 1989

- Played Mini-Satellite Tours in India 1990, Mexico 1991, Canada 2004

- Won Men's Singles, National American Indian Championships 1989, 1996

- Winner, Men's 35 Singles Fiesta Bowl Scottsdale Open, 2003

- Semifinalist, National Indoor Championships, 2003

- Semifinalist, National Grass Court Championships, 2003

- Won two grass court tournaments in England, 2003

- Nationally Ranked: Men's 35 Singles #5 in the U.S., #11 in the World Internationally, 2003

- Member, Italia Cup Team, USTA Men's 35 International Team. Represented the United States in Antalya, Turkey. ITF Men's 35 Doubles Champions, 2004 (Partner Henry Karrasch).

Gerald Tuckwin

GERALD L. "JERRY" TUCKWIN
Inducted 2009

DATE OF BIRTH: February 14, 1942

BIRTH PLACE: Mayetta, Kansas

TRIBE: Prairie Band Potawatomi

EDUCATION: Haskell Institute (High School), Lawrence, Kansas 1960

    University of Wichita, Bachelor Degree, 1964

    University of Arizona, Masters in Education, 1970

SPORTS DATA: Track – Cross Country Coaching

ACHIEVEMENTS:

- Track and Field, Cross Country and Marathon Coach at Haskell Indian Junior College and Haskell Indian Nations University, Coach Tuckwin's athletes were named All-Americans a total of thirty times.

    Track and Field – 14

    Cross Country – 9

    Marathon – 7

* The Marathon team won 2 National Championships

- Coach Tuckwin was the National Junior College Athletic Association Cross Country Coach of the year two times!

SPECIAL AND HONORED INDUCTEES

1926 Haskell Football

HASKELL'S UNDEFEATED 1926 FOOTBALL SQUAD

Front Row: Elijah Smith, Oneida; Louis Colby, Klamath; Louis Jennings, Cherokee; George Levi, Arapaho; Theodore "Tiny" Roebuck, Choctaw; R.E. "Dick" Hanley, Head Coach; Tom Stidham, Creek; Mayes McLain, Cherokee; Egbert Ward, Yakima; Albert Hawley, Gros Ventre; Simon Gurneau, Chippewa.

Second Row: L.B. "Pat" Hanley, Assistant Coach; Lehman Brightman, Creek; Hubert McKenzie, Cherokee; David Ward, Yakima; David Bible, Creek; Theodore Sallee, Washoe; Joe Pappio, Chippewa; Harry Jones, Sioux; Clyde Fairbanks, Chippewa; Joe Cross, Caddo; Worth Calvert, Cherokee; A.R. Stark, Reserve Coach.

Third Row: James Grant, Chippewa; Sundie Swimmers, Cherokee; Eugehe Fritz, Cherokee; Philip Types, Nez Perce; Mr. Smith, Reporter AP; Peter Johns, Oneida; Peter Nevada, Paiute; Frank Giroux, Sioux; Henry Reed, Ute; (Not shown Tola Pierce, Seneca.

1926 HASKELL FOOTBALL TEAM

The football season of 1926 was unquestionably the most significant in the history of Haskell's gridiron competition, if not, indeed, in the whole history of the Indian race. It saw at Haskell the dedication of the first and only Indian stadium, and at the same time produced the strongest football team which ever brought glory and fame to the Purple and Gold.

It brought to Haskell one of the country's eight undefeated teams, an aggregation which battled its way from gridiron to gridiron, meeting every style of football known, with added honors upon each appearance. It emerged from a rugged season of thirteen games, having won twelve contests and tied one, and to give the world Mayes McLain, highest point scorer – 259 points – it has ever known, the highest scoring team of the year – 559 to opponent's 63 – and the widest traveled team of the year – coast to coast by railroad Pullman car.

From the moment the football squad began training in August, 1926, the dedication of the new stadium loomed in the offing, casting a shadow of unusual responsibility upon the team – a responsibility these young Indians willingly accepted. This bred a "winning" spirit which lasted throughout the season.

The Indians were up to the proper edge for the important stadium dedication game against the "Bisons" of Bucknell University on October 30th. This game will ever stand out in the memories of those who witnessed the first Home-Coming Game the Indians ever played in their own arena.

The Indian Braves swarmed over Bucknell like pirates boarding a treasure ship. The three thousand Indians in the stands and the thousands of white football enthusiasts were treated to a football exhibition which was letter perfect. The Indians stopped the Bison attack time after time before it could be fairly launched. On the other hand, dazzling runs by the Braves sent the score higher and higher until the count was 36 to 0 at the end of the contest. Elijah Smith was the hero of the contest with his seventy-five yard dash through the line of scrimmage for a touchdown. Ward's generalship and interference was great. McLain, Levi, and all backs indulged in plain and fancy running. The performance of the entire squad was the eloquent expression of thanks on the part of Haskell Institute and its student body to the older Indian Chiefs and Tribal Leaders who made all contributions necessary to build the stadium.

1926 SEASON'S RESULTS

Date	Opponents	Haskell	Opponent
Sept. 18	Drury College at Lawrence	65	0
Sept. 25	Univ. of Wichita, at Wichita.	57	0
Oct. 1	Des Moines Still College at Lawrence	55	0
Oct. 9	Morningside College at Lawrence	38	0
Oct. 16	Dayton University at Dayton	30	14
Oct. 21	Jackson University at Lawrence	95	0
Oct. 30	Bucknell University at Lawrence	36	0

Nov. 6   Loyola Univ.of Chicago at Kansas City, Missouri

                                          27   7

Nov. 13 Boston College at Boston, Mass.   21   21

Nov. 20 Michigan Aggies at Lansing, Michigan 40   7

Nov. 25 St. Xavier at Cincinnati, Ohio   27   0

Dec. 4   Tulsa University at Tulsa, Oklahoma 27   7

Dec. 18 Hawaiian All-Stars at San Francisco, California

                                          40   7

HONORARY INDUCTEES

● LOUIS R. BRUCE - 1973

Mr. Bruce is of Mohawk-Sioux ancestry. He is the former US Commissioner of Indian Affairs whose full support of Robert L. Bennett's Hall of Fame conceptual ideas, proceeded with the establishment of the American Indian Athletic Hall of Fame and the first Hall of Fame Induction of November 25, 1972 in Lawrence, Kansas.

He is the recipient of the American Indian Achievement Award and the Freedoms award for "Outstanding Contributions in Promoting the American Way of Life".

● ROBERT L. BENNETT -1977

Mr. Bennett was enshrined in the Indian Athletic Hall of Fame on December 3, 1977 at ceremonies held on the Haskell campus. The Indian Athletic Hall was founded while Bennett was commissioner of the Bureau of Indian Affairs.

● FRANK W. "MAC" MC DONALD - 1978

In recognition of his foresight and commitment to the building of a stadium to meet the needs of the student body at Haskell Institute, and his dedication to service to that institution and Indian people. Enshrined on December 9, 1978.

● GEORGE P. LAVATTA - 1981

Enshrined on March 28, 1981 for his service and loyalty to the American Indian Athletic Hall of Fame. Served as the first Chairman of the Board of Directors for the Hall of Fame, 1972. .

● TURNER A. COCHRAN - 1982

An outstanding Alumnus of Haskell Institute, and is a member of the Board of Regents of Haskell Indian Junior College. He is a Caddo/ Chickasaw/Cherokee tribesman. There have been five enshrinement ceremonies planned and accomplished during his tenure as the coordinator and executive secretary of the American Indian Athletic Hall of Fame (1982).

● SIDNEY M. "SID" CARNEY - 1985

In recognition of his vision and leadership in nurturing the growth of the American Indian Athletic Hall of Fame, his significant role in elevating Haskell Institute to a comprehensive Junior College, and his commitment of the welfare and happiness of Indian People. Enshrined on March 30, 1985.

● WALLACE E. "WALLY" GALLUZZI - 1989

Enshrined in the American Indian Athletic Hall of Fame March 21, 1987. In recognition of his philosophy of academic and athletic excellence for Indian youth, and his service and devotion to the development of the American Indian Athletic Hall of Fame.

NOMINATION
INFORMATION

Instructions for Completing Nomination Form

Election for enshrinement into the Hall of Fame is based on achievement as a performing athlete or in other fields of athletics **beyond the high school level**. Contributions to the Indian Community, ones character as well as ones success in their chosen profession is also considered.

Once a candidate qualifies on basic criteria, namely: Proven membership in a recognized Indian Tribe, Exceptional Achievement in Athletics in a sport recognized world wide, each member of the Board of Directors evaluates the candidate's application.

Nomination Instructions

1. Both male and female athletes may be nominated.

2. Indian athletes who are living, deceased, active or retired may be nominated.

3. The Tribe or the federal government (BIA) must certify nominees' membership in a federally recognized tribe. This proof must accompany the nomination forms.

4. A 5x7 black and white photo of Nominee in his/her sport uniform must also be submitted with the Nomination Form.

5. Newspaper clippings, statistical data, record book documentation or other pertinent data reflecting outstanding sports/athletic achievements, honor, awards, i.e., All-American, All-Conference, All-Pro Team Selection, Olympic team selection/participation or National Sports Award. Sport(s) must be recognized by AAU, NCAA, and NAIA or has had National or International recognition. Athletic Achievement of the **High School level will not be considered.**

6. Should Certificates, Medals, Ribbons, Plaques, etc., be submitted, they will be returned via Certified Mail immediately after examination by the Board of Directors.

7. Good documentation of athletic achievements is essential for proper evaluation.

8. Names, addresses and phone numbers of 4 or 5 persons who knew the nominee well – athletically or professionally.

9. Completed Nomination Forms with supporting documentation should be forwarded for consideration by the Board at a regularly scheduled meeting for that purpose. Please send to: Dr. Holly Mullan, Executive Secretary, 1827 East Saint Charles, Phoenix, Arizona, 85042.

10. **Non Refundable Application fee is $50.00,** which should be sent in with application. No application will be considered without fee.

American Indian Athletic Hall of Fame
EXECUTIVE OFFICE: 1827 East Saint Charles,
Phoenix, AZ 85042
Phone: 602-276-3201 Fax: 602-276-3325
Email: indianhalloffame@hotmail.com

AMERICAN INDIAN ATHLETIC HALL OF FAME

NOMINATION FORM

PERSONAL DATA

Name _____ Date of Birth _____

Address _____ Date of Death _____

City _____ State _____ Zip Code _____

Tribe _____ Degree of Indian Blood _____

Address to verify Degree of Indian Blood

_____

FAMILY DATA

Name of Father _____ Telephone #: _____

Address _____ City _____

State _____ Zip Code _____

Name of Mother _____ Telephone #: _____

Address _____ City _____

State _____ Zip Code _____

Names of Brothers and Sisters, Address and Telephone Number:

_____

_____

_____

_____

EDUCATION DATA

Name of High School and Year Graduated:

Name(s) of Universities/College: Year(s) Attended:

Degree: _____ Year Graduated: _____

SPORTS DATA

Sport(s) Lettered In: Year(s) Lettered:

Sports Played (Amateur/Professional). Please summarize athletic achievements and year. Additional information may be furnished on plain bond paper.

Recognitions(s), Honors and Awards Received: Year:

OTHER DATA

Summarize professional, civic and community organization(s) achievements (especially in the Indian Communities) extra pages may be used if needed:

Nominated By:

Name _____ Date _____

Address _____

City _____ State _____ Zip Code _____

Telephone Number

_____

About The Author

Ms. Holly Mullan, Ed.D. was attending Haskell Indian Junior College when the American Indian Athletic Hall of Fame began. Being a Native American (Cherokee, Quapaw and Euchee) gave her special interest in the Hall of Fame from its inception. Ms. Mullan participated on the Men's Tennis Team while attending Haskell. She continued her education at the University of Kansas receiving her Bachelors degree and continued her education at Emporia State University to receive her Master's degree.

Dr. Mullan worked in Indian Education for a number of years following her fathers lead. Her father Dr. Noah Allen was Athletic Director at Haskell Indian Junior College in 1972 and assisted with the first induction ceremony for the American Indian Athletic Hall of Fame. Dr. Mullan has been the Executive Secretary for the Hall of Fame since 2004.

After serving in the field of education for thirty years Ms. Mullan received her Doctors Degree in Education from Arizona State University. She is currently the Superintendent of her own charter school in Scottsdale, Arizona.

Index